Advance Praise for *Calling B*

"My mother always said, 'If it's important to you, you'll find the time. If it's not, you'll find an excuse.' Time is the only commodity in life that *is* fair. We are all given 24 hours every day, and if you're using the 'I'm too busy' excuse, then either you really don't want to do it or you need to read Andrew's book. You will be given a roadmap to success that will change your relationship with time so you can finally get things done!"
—Chef AJ, bestselling author and host of the daily YouTube show *Chef AJ LIVE!*

"Andrew has shown me, as a journalist who is always looking for more hours in a day, how to boldly create order and happiness. He is honest, up-front and forever the source I turn to when it comes to clarity and time management!"
—Tamsen Fadal, Emmy-award-winning journalist and author

"Andrew Mellen previously asked Americans to examine their emotional relationship to stuff—and now he is working his magic with time. Successful, happy people have plenty of leisure time because they know how to spend it wisely. This book is a rallying cry for people to take back control of their time *and* their lives. It could not have come at a more opportune moment in our culture, as people around the world re-evaluate their relationship to both work and money."
—Quentin Fottrell, *MarketWatch*'s Managing Editor–Personal Finance and The Moneyist columnist

"Nothing breaks my heart like hearing that a new acquaintance "would love to travel but just can never find the time" (something I hear all the time when I'm introduced as a travel expert). Andrew Mellen's superb new book calls BS on that excuse, and gives actionable, straightforward smart advice on how to make time work for you . . . rather than the other way around. Read this book and you'll

be able to find that, yes, you do have time to travel, and to do the other meaningful, non–work-related activities in your life. Small shifts in outlook can create a bonanza of free time. And what could be better than that?"
—Pauline Frommer, Co-President of the Frommer's guidebooks and Frommers.com

"*Calling Bullsh*t on Busy* is an invaluable resource to help you make progress toward achieving your aspirations. Andrew Mellen provides countless insightful ideas, such as disabling distracting social media platforms and curbing time-thieving procrastination habits. As a photo archivist, I wish all those who have collected photo memories over the years, tucked away in albums and boxes, gathering dust, would make use of his uncluttering advice and digitally preserve their treasured photo memories. This clever book will be one you find yourself coming back to again and again."
—Mitch Goldstone, CEO, ScanMyPhotos.com

"Andrew Mellen has been assisting my organization for years with his no-nonsense and humorous approach to efficiency. Andrew's latest book not only is entertaining and engaging but will provide the reader with new insight, which will undoubtedly change their concept of time management."
—Marcia Griffin, CEO and founder, HomeFree-USA

"As a couples therapist for the last 20 years, I've helped fix thousands of relationships. And I can honestly say when it comes to working on your relationship with 'time,' there's no better expert than Andrew Mellen."
—Ian Kerner, *New York Times* bestselling author of *She Comes First* and TED 2021 speaker

"From the very first page, I was laughing and learning. As someone who has read a lot of books about 'time management,' I was stunned by how fast Andrew could shift my story about time. This is the book we all need. Loved it!"
—Jennifer Louden, national bestselling author of *Why Bother? Discover the Desire for What's Next* and *The Woman's Comfort Book*

"*Calling Bullsh*t on Busy* is the book we all need right now. Andrew Mellen explodes every time-worn, overly complicated approach to time management—and in their place, he lays out practical, empowering methods that actually work. Armed with his signature wit and vivid, compelling examples, he's written a wonderfully accessible guide that pulled me through its pages, gave me tools I could instantly employ, and will forever change how I think about time. Mind blown!"
—Michael MacLennan, TV writer and creator of *Bomb Girls* and Netflix's *Tiny Pretty Things*

"Most people have no idea how important every choice about time is to the quality of their lives. To truly understand that impact, you must read this book. I love how Mellen guides the reader to fully participate, inviting them to bring both heart and spirit into their work and live their best life. Uniquely and cleverly done."
—Peggy McColl, *New York Times* bestselling author of *Your Destiny Switch*

"With this book you will finally be free from the mindset issues that plague even the highest performers. Mellen puts you back in the driver's seat of life and has you enjoying the entire ride!"
—Mike Michalowicz, author of *Profit First* and *Clockwork*

"As someone who does creative work, I fear that time management systems will kill inspiration—but what I found with Andrew Mellen's new book was the opposite. It showed me how to liberate it. Beware: he will not accept any of your excuses! Which is actually doing you a huge favor. If you're ready to create order in your everyday life, hour by hour, this book is for you."
—Susan Piver, *New York Times* bestselling author of *The Four Noble Truths of Love* and *The Buddhist Enneagram*

"Andrew Mellen calls BS on anyone wanting better time management. In *Calling Bullsh*t on Busy* he writes in an engaging, entertaining, and truly honest way about how we view time, how we waste time, and why we blame a clock for our own behaviors! Refreshing and probing, it is a book for anyone who needs more time."
—Sharon Salzberg, *New York Times* bestselling author of *Lovingkindness* and *Real Happiness*

"When asked what's most important in someone's life, they'll often cite relationships. And yet so many of us prioritize other things. Andrew's book is a wake-up call to those pressing snooze on their lives and who miss important events, relationships and experiences in favor of being 'too busy.' With tough love and actionable steps, this book guides readers to use their time wisely and in a way that ultimately serves their deepest values."
—Andrea Syrtash, relationship expert and author of *He's Just Not Your Type (And That's A Good Thing)*

"If you struggle with ADHD like me, this step-by-step approach provides an invaluable toolkit that can help reframe the way you think about time management. With his easy-to-follow instructions and tips, you'll be able to take control of your days and achieve much more than you ever thought possible."
—Sharon Vinderine, CEO of Parent Tested Parent Approved and television lifestyle expert

"We all know that wasted time is one of the worst kinds of clutter. Add in negative self-talk and excuses, and is it any wonder so many of us are overwhelmed and constantly complaining about being too busy?! That's where Andrew Mellen's new book is so smart—it immediately blows up the lies we tell ourselves and then lovingly (and fiercely) replaces them with instantly actionable strategies and steps you can take now to get those hours back and more. Read this book and change your entire relationship with time today!"
—Peter Walsh, professional organizer and *New York Times* bestselling author of *It's All Too Much*

"In Zen, busy-ness is viewed as a form of mind-less-ness rather than mind-full-ness. Andrew Mellen wisely speaks to how our relationship with our own minds and internal narratives determines our relationship not only with time but with the world around us. By changing the way we think and act in regard to time, we discover a greater sense of ease and freedom inside and out. *Calling Bullsh*t on Busy* offers no-nonsense, values-based, and simple yet transformative tools and practices for bringing us into the present moment with clear intention, gratitude, and abundance. And it does so with a healthy dose of humor!"
—Tenzen David Zimmerman, Central Abbot, San Francisco Zen Center

CALLING
BULLSH*T
ON **BUSY**

CALLING
BULLSH*T
ON BUSY

A practical guide to ditching the time management
myth and quickly achieving your goals

Andrew Mellen

Author of *Wall Street Journal* bestseller *Unstuff Your Life!*

First Line Press

cbobbook.com

St. Petersburg, FL, USA

Library of Congress Control Number: 2023930479

Paperback ISBN: 979-8-9874774-0-3

E-Book ISBN: 979-8-9874774-1-0

Also available in audiobook.

Cover and text design by Kristy Twellmann Hill

Art direction by fleck creative studio

Contents

Introduction

Thank you for picking up this book. May I pay you back with a no-bullshit piece of honesty right away, please?

Time management is a myth.

Sorry! It would be great if you could just wrestle time to the ground and force it to behave. I want that so much for you . . . almost as much as I want it for myself.

But, unfortunately, neither of us will win that fight.

We might as well rip the Band-Aid off and get right to it.

Your time is precious and if you're going to invest any of it in reading this book, you should get some serious ROI right from the get-go.

So here's the big takeaway: time management doesn't exist.

No one can teach you how to manage time—no one. Not David Allen, Brian Tracy, Ken Blanchard, Stephen Covey, or *insert name of time management guru here*. What you *can* learn is how to manage *yourself* in relation to time.

So this is really more of a relationship book.

The good news is, you won't find a bunch of unicorns, heart emojis, or affirmations here to inspire you to fall in love with time. You also won't find a bunch of complicated systems that take more time to set up and run than they ever save.

No doubt you've felt at times like time is cruel, but the truth is that time is indifferent to you—which may feel worse than if time were actually out to get you.

Time does exactly what time does—tick on, minute by minute, hour by hour, day by day. Either you have to get on board with that concept, or you are going to Don Quixote yourself into some serious anger and frustration.

That's one of the reasons I wrote this book.

Because in the 26+ years that I've been speaking, teaching, and coaching, I've seen an incredibly large number of people, including some of my friends, colleagues, and mentors, trying to win an unwinnable fight.

All that grief, anger, and disappointment ends up self-directed—like if you were only better or smarter, you'd crack this code.

But the problem is, there is no time "code" to crack. The problem is you.

Or, more specifically, *how you think about, feel about, and interact with time.*

Everything in this book is about managing your own actions, not about managing time.

Also, this book is not going to teach you how to get other people to better manage *their* time.

If they have a problem, get them their own copy of this book. You won't find passive-aggressive techniques you can use to subtly manipulate other people into changing their behaviors—when have you ever seen that work anyway?

So . . . what gives me the right to be the big buzz-kill smart-ass who's trying to blow up the concept of time management?

Well, according to the media, I'm the most organized man in America. I've already written a *Wall Street Journal* (and Audible) best-selling book, *Unstuff Your Life!*.

And as an author, educator, speaker, and organizational evangelist, I've spent decades working with individuals and companies around the world, helping them become more organized, effective, and efficient.

Just like we do with clutter, when solving productivity issues, we look for bottlenecks and points of friction in our clients' lives and businesses and remove them as quickly as possible.

Those clients run the gamut from formerly crazy-busy CEOs to seriously overworked executive assistants, and from award-winning authors, designers, and filmmakers to stay-at-home parents and homemakers. (These last two don't get many awards, but they should.)

From solopreneurs to Fortune 50 companies, and from tiny nonprofits to megachurches, what does every one of these clients have in common? A belief that there is too much to do, and not enough time to do it.

If you read that and think, "But Andrew, that's *my* problem, too! I have too much to do and not enough time!" this book is for you.

Because you, too, are laboring under the faulty belief that you are exceptional or even unique . . . and sadly, you are not. *When it comes to time, that is.*

Almost every productivity client I've ever had has shown up with some version of tear-your-hair-out anxiety or depression or mania, convinced that *they* are the *worst* time manager in human history.

While that is not true, what these clients may all have in common is a secret inner drama queen.

So, whether they are

- chronically late procrastinators and poor planners
- conflict-averse people pleasers
- creative daydreamers and artists
- captains of industry surrounded by "incompetent" teams
- competitive athletes or entrepreneurs looking for a secret edge
- committee-rich volunteers, socialites, or philanthropists
- competent but overwhelmed first responders at the end of their ropes, or
- someone just like you,

they all come to me with a version of the same story.

No one else has *their* problems, and if we did, we would understand exactly why they can't show up on time, meet deadlines, get enough rest, or accomplish any other time-specific thing.

By the time my clients are finished working with me, each of those stories is dismantled as the fiction it is.

Sure, there's a kernel of truth in most of their stories—there are demands on their time. But the story is almost always worse than the reality.

And, of course, some teams do suck. Some employees and colleagues are awful. Some life circumstances are intense and seemingly relentless.

But . . . mostly they just are what they are.

The real problems are more likely an unhealthy corporate culture, bad work habits, no SOPs (standard operating procedures), wobbly or absent accountability, unclear communication, hidden agendas, personality conflicts, or an unwillingness to say no. Time has little or nothing to do with any of those things.

So when we look at who's responsible for creating or maintaining these faulty conditions, we quickly see that they—my clients—are.

That's why we blow up their stories. We *must* get to the root cause of where this narrative comes from so we can wipe the slate clean and build from the ground up.

And that new foundation is built on one's core values—those things that matter so much to you that you'd rather die than surrender them.

From there, we construct a morning routine that ensures shit gets done.

And we're talking about the important stuff that makes a difference in our lives—not ridiculous busywork that matters to no one, or frivolous time wasters like posting your latest breakfast burrito on Instagram.

These people (re)discover their priorities and, more importantly, how to make daily choices based on those priorities instead of kicking them down the road for "later." *You know, when you have more time.*

They learn about the 8 Deadly Time Thieves and how to neutralize them. In order, they are Interruptions, Multitasking, Overcommitting, Poor Planning, Email, Meetings, Social Media, and Procrastination.

As a result, they start sleeping better, have more confidence, and feel in control of their lives.

They may not be able to control a pandemic, but they now get the important things done first—when it matters. And after that, they don't waste time worrying about things they can't control.

Sound impossible? It isn't.

Imagine starting each day with clarity about what you need to do and how and when you'll do it.

Imagine being on time for every appointment, getting enough sleep, and feeling in control of your life.

Imagine never again feeling like you're being dragged behind your day like it's a 100-pound dog chasing a squirrel up and down a tree.

You, too, can become the captain of your days, weeks, months, and years. I've seen it happen thousands of times, at every income level and job title, and in every country.

Of course, there is work to be done to get those results.

Reading this book is a great start, and it will definitely help with your mindset . . . but the real work begins when you put the book down and start changing your behavior.

That's when things really take off.

Here's a fact: even though I may not know you yet, I want the best for you and I want you to succeed. So I will coach you and cheer you on from these pages. And I'll make it super clear what you need to do to change your mindset and conquer each time thief.

I'll show you again and again that lying to yourself about how busy you are is undermining every other thing you do, from the moment you open your eyes until your head hits the pillow at night.

And if you want these results, you'll take the suggestions and implement them.

Hopefully you already feel somewhere deep inside of you that you and the people you love are worth fighting for and that things can change—even if you don't yet know how.

And that's a great place to begin. From there, we can go anywhere . . . so let's start with this concept first.

THE CLOCK IS NOT YOUR PROBLEM

Have you ever felt like everyone else has more time than you do?

Sure, *they* can read 50+ books a year, exercise 7 days a week, finish work in time to cook a gourmet meal and still enjoy date night out with their spouse. That's because they don't have your life, your job, your responsibilities, your kids, your house, your . . . *fill in the blank here,* right?

If they did, just like you, they would *not* have time for all those activities.

Now, in rare instances, your time *is* all spoken for. You'll meet one of my clients whose life really is that full.

But for most of us, it's bullshit.

We all get the same 60 minutes an hour, 24 hours a day, and 8,760 hours a year. No more, no less. So the clock *can't* be your problem, because it's ticking the same way for all of us.

The reason your colleague gets *so* much more done than you do, even with a new baby at home and hours spent volunteering at the local animal shelter, isn't *time*. It's how they *spend* their time.

In other words: *you* are your problem, not the clock.

If that upsets you, sit with it for a moment. It's not going to kill you, and it just might set you free from every other piece of bullshit you've fed yourself over the years.

But don't wallow.

This isn't an invitation to fall down the rabbit hole of feeling sorry for yourself and start a litany of every reason why you're such a loser that this book will work for everyone *except* you. That's just more bullshit.

Remember, you're not special . . . not in the ways you think you are. The good news is, you're probably quite special in ways you haven't even seen yet.

Feeling shame over past mistakes is not your ticket out. Taking responsibility for where you are and making new choices is.

Because here's a news flash: you aren't broken, and you are *not* the worst. What ails you is entirely fixable.

We'll talk more in the next chapter about why some of us *like* to feel broken—how feeling damaged enables us to bail on ourselves in big and small ways. But for now, all you need to know is that you are your problem—and you can change.

You don't have to sit on a cushion lotus-style or become a vegan or run an Ironman to do it, either. Although once you read this book, you may discover you have the desire—not to mention the time—to do any or all of those things.

But first, we need to look at the 200 lies you tell yourself every day.[1]

THE POWER OF STORY

If you read my first book, *Unstuff Your Life!*, you know that I talk a lot about story. Specifically, the stories we tell ourselves—and choose to believe as fact. Story is just as influential when it comes to time as it is to organization, so we'll be talking about it a lot here, too.

There's also a bit of math, but simple math, like the kind that lets you count your change back from a dollar—we're not talking calculus or trigonometry.

Change your relationship with story and with math, and time management becomes incredibly easy.

Oh, and this book's aim is not to turn you into a hyperproductive, robotic, soulless tasking machine—unless that is *your* goal, too. Otherwise, you're going to remain surprisingly human.

You're going to learn how to live your best life—whatever that means to you—and to participate fully, show up fiercely, and bring your whole heart and spirit to whatever you're engaged in at any given moment.

And that includes your relationships with the two key players in this book: time and the clock.

You can certainly use these techniques to conquer the world and become the next Rhianna, but as fabulous as she is, why would you want to when you can just be the best version of you?

These methods can also improve the quality of your life, reduce stress, and help you use your time effectively. You can live a life you're proud of, and one that impacts others on any scale you choose.

You don't have to use these techniques to cure cancer. It can be enough to just be a good parent, partner, or friend. Show up fully, love expansively, and pick up after yourself—none of which are that complicated.

SPEAKING OF LIFE AND LOVE . . .

I don't want to be morbid, but you are going to die. I don't know when—I'm not psychic—but we're all getting kicked off the island at some point.

Since none of us knows exactly when that's going to happen, I don't want you (or anyone else) getting to the end of this experience thinking, "Crap! I want a do-over. This is not how I wanted this to play out . . ."

That would suck. So let's avoid that and create a different outcome instead.

First, we need to acknowledge that there are things you need to do to keep life moving forward, and not all of them spark joy.

The basic administration of your life and your family probably requires going to the grocery store, paying bills, mowing the lawn, taking out the trash, doing laundry, and lots of other stuff that isn't especially fulfilling . . . just necessary.

If you can afford to delegate some or all of those tasks, you're ahead of the game. For the rest of us, those tasks need to be streamlined and completed as efficiently as possible.

You could also strip all those things out of your life and become a digital nomad or minimalist, or move into a tiny house.

Any of these choices will definitely reduce the external demands on your time. But they're not required—you can have a simple streamlined life with plenty of possessions and domestic commitments.

Then there's work. If you're trading time for money, that too needs to become far more efficient than it probably is right now.

There's also what we think of as "free" time—the time we spend with family, on vacation, at parties, on our phones, or enjoying dinner with friends.

In each of these categories, you have agency . . . even if you don't currently *feel* like you do.

And that's what this book is going to teach you—how to leverage every minute in each category so that you're using your time strategically and investing it in the things that have the greatest impact on your life and the lives of your loved ones.

WHAT'S IMPORTANT TO YOU?

Which activities in your life have the greatest impact on you and everyone you're connected to?

This isn't a rhetorical or trick question, and it's not absent-minded navel-gazing.

If you don't know what's important, you will almost always be distracted by what's urgent.

Have you ever met someone you were *really* into? Or found a new hobby that absorbed you from day one? I don't care how busy you say you are—time magically opens up when there's something you *really* want to do.

On the flip side, it's tough to find time for the stuff we *don't* want to do, like writing a term paper or cleaning the house, even when we "know better." Suddenly, we have "no time" again.

Funny, right?

Not really. It's easier to find time for the stuff we care about. The stuff we want to do doesn't feel like work—or at least it feels like rewarding work and not a waste of time. We don't need motivation to do *that* stuff—it generates its own momentum and feeds us.

And that's where our values come in.

One key to increasing productivity is leveraging your values—using them to get you off the sofa or social media.

So the first step in your time/self-management journey will be this: figuring out what matters most to you. Because that will be your North Star, constantly orienting you toward the things you need to do and also want to do.

Many of us "manage" our time by jumping into the next task that shows up in front of us, whether or not it's important or even makes sense. We work at it until we get bored, distracted, or pulled in another direction.

If you've ever spent an entire day tasking away and felt like you had nothing to show for all that effort, you get what I'm talking about.

You can't prioritize without priorities.

Once you've got them, it's easy to rank tasks from the things that matter most down to the things that don't matter at all. And if the tasks at the bottom of that list don't get done—and they probably won't—that's okay, because the important stuff did.

No one else can tell you what is important, even though lots of people may try.

Your values won't match mine, your neighbor's, or anyone else's. So, you won't find morning routine lists in this book filled with specifics like "Do 10 inverted pushups," or "Drink 12 ounces of ice water," or "Cold-call 5 prospects."

The principles I'm sharing with you are universal, but their application is highly specific to you and your values. Cookie-cutter checklists give you a false sense of hope that if you master someone else's values, your life will get better. Not likely.

Mastering my *own* values is how I changed my life.

I was laid off in Seattle in 1996, where I had been recruited two years earlier to run a small theater. It was a humbling and humiliating experience. I found out I no longer had a job when I showed up for work one morning and discovered that, while I had been at rehearsal the night before, the locks to our office had been changed.

A mentor once told me that inside every disappointment is the seed of an equal or greater opportunity. I needed to believe that was true that morning.

I spent six months in Seattle collecting unemployment benefits and looking for another job. I got a lot of sympathy and exactly zero offers for work. And then an old acquaintance invited me to co-produce an awards ceremony with him at the Kennedy Center in Washington, DC.

Saying yes to that offer was the beginning of my next career, although I didn't know it at the time. I thought it was just another gig.

Being of service has been one of my core values since I was in college. I wasn't viewing this assignment through that lens then, but looking back now, I can see that not only that event but the work I started taking on following that event was all about being of service.

It was also a way to pay my bills, but I could just as easily have done that in a restaurant rather than starting a business as a professional organizer.

I kept applying for work as a nonprofit arts administrator, but this other work kept coming and coming, and I could see the impact I was having on my clients' lives.

And I remember very clearly standing outside my sixth-floor walk-up apartment in Manhattan and making the decision to pursue this work full-time. I had no idea then that I would become "The Most Organized Man in America," or that I'd have the privilege of speaking and teaching around the globe.

I've achieved things through this work that I couldn't have imagined then. I've been invited to work with the Metropolitan Museum of Art, the New York Mets, and Goldman Sachs. And I've spoken at Dwell on Design, BlogHer, and the Great British Business Show to standing-room-only crowds.

I've written for O, The Oprah Magazine and Real Simple, and published my first book with Penguin Random House.

All because of some luck, some hard work, and making choices aligned with my values.

None of this makes me special. And if I can do it, you can, too. While these may be exceptional results, I believe they are possible for you, too, when you make choices aligned with your values.

So, in this book, we'll focus on two major actions. Each one of these will change your life on its own. Together, they make you unstoppable:

- Ditching the lies, bullshit, and baggage that hold you back while they seem to be serving you—they aren't.
- Focusing your time on your wildly important goals—which you will define and clarify as part of the process—and hacking every recurring task in your life for maximum efficiency with minimal effort.

If that doesn't sound revolutionary or transformative enough, you can go right back to the anxious, constantly late, overworked, and compromised life you were living before you picked up this book. It's waiting for you with open arms, promising that things will be different next time.

If you *do* want more time and freedom in your life, please read on.

WHY IS THIS BOOK DIFFERENT?

Maybe because I'm the first person who has told you that time management doesn't even exist . . . ?

This book is different from any other book about time you've *ever* read, for five reasons:

REASON 1: NO BULLSHIT

I'm a New Yorker at heart, even though I grew up in Detroit—and both places have shaped the way I define determination, grit, and success.

Some people think New Yorkers are rude, but we're not. We're direct. The pace of the city won't tolerate bullshit. There are so many inherent obstacles to doing anything in New York that wasted time costs twice as much here.

My frank way of speaking could be termed "tough love," but I think of it as simple honesty. I respect you and your time enough to not waste it trying to manage your feelings. We'll dive deep into truths that may be hard to hear but are critical for recovering your time and getting you where you want to go, as fast as you want to travel.

REASON 2: MATH, NOT STORY

If the word "math" freaks you out, don't panic. As long as you graduated from the third grade, you can do the kind of math I'm talking about: simple addition and subtraction. One of the goals of this book is to pry you loose from the clutches of story and introduce you to a facts-based approach to life—and that isn't possible without a little bit of math.

Here's what I mean:

You have 24 hours per day, just like the rest of us. If you spend 8 of those hours sleeping, you now have 16 hours awake to manage.

If you spend 8 hours at work, 2 hours commuting, 1 hour exercising, and 2 hours preparing and eating meals, simple math tells us there's no way you can spend 4 hours a day pursuing a graduate degree. Or bingeing 4 episodes of your favorite TV show . . .

Because $16 - 8 - 2 - 1 - 2 = 3$.

See? The math doesn't add up.

You have 3 hours per day to work with, not 4.

And if you spend the bulk of those 3 hours on life admin tasks like errands and washing up, and the rest on semiconscious activities like wandering around, arguing, complaining, surfing the internet, etc., you can see how little flexible time you actually have without making different choices.

You might want to fall back into a story to "explain" why you don't have more time. Something like, "I'm just not good at managing my time. I'm really creative but I can't seem to find enough hours in the day to study, play with my kids, read Spider-Man comics, etc."

But the fundamental math is the problem because you never *had* four hours to begin with. The best productivity expert in the world can't create more hours for you.

So you can either subtract time from existing activities or adjust your expectations—it's as simple as that.

Thanks, math!

REASON 3: A SYSTEM THAT IS THE ABSENCE OF A SYSTEM

I know . . . so meta.

There are no complicated organizational methods or systems in this book. There are plenty of time management books out there that demand you adopt an elaborate, complex, or *time-consuming* system—which eats up more time than it delivers back.

Those systems make no sense, regardless of how well they are packaged. We can applaud their marketing prowess even while poking a hole in their logic. If you're saving 45 minutes a day by spending an hour managing your system, you just lost 15 minutes—that's a horrible ROI.

Your time is too valuable to waste on managing another system. That's why there's no special software and no patented tools to buy. Just universal principles that are easy to understand and use so you can heal your relationship with time.

And exactly three tools are required—which you already have if you own a smartphone, and they're cheap if you don't:

- A timer
- A stopwatch
- A calendar

That's it. Not a *specific* timer, stopwatch, or calendar . . . you don't need a timer shaped like a tomato unless you want one.

You need a way to count down time, add up time, and make appointments with yourself.

So go high tech, low tech, or no tech with your tools. As long as you consistently apply the principles, you'll see the results.

REASON 4: ACTION- AND RESULTS-ORIENTED

Every chapter finishes with a "bottom line" summation followed by a chapter recap and fast-action steps you can take to recapture one or more hours per week. You're not reading this book for fun—though I hope you enjoy it.

So theoretically you could just read those and get to work.

You will also find these recaps and lots of free bonus materials at www. cbobbook.com if you want them digitally.

Of course, there are other things to glean from the book by reading it all the way through. And remember, any tool without a new mindset is likely to fail or not be sustainable. That's why you should read the book cover to cover, and then go back to attack specific problems more thoroughly.

REASON 5: NO BULLSHIT . . . AGAIN

I can't stress this enough—if you're looking for someone to cosign your bullshit, this book is going to make you crazy.

If, instead, you are hungry for another way to live that feels better and gets you off that hamster wheel of "busy" for good, you're in the right place.

Your stories suck—you don't. The world doesn't suck and you're not a victim of circumstances. None of your stories automatically disqualify you from increasing your productivity and getting more time into your days.

You are not special when it comes to time. And that is what is going to set you free.

REAL-LIFE TIME WARRIORS

To help you identify where you're at right now, and to break up any feelings of isolation or uniqueness, please meet three clients of mine. See if you identify with any of them.

PATSY

Patsy is a working mother with two young kids. When she came to me, she was exhausted and pretty beaten up by life.

Her typical response to anything new, good or bad, was defeated anger . . . or angry defeat.

As if one more piece of crap heading her way was going to be the piece of crap that broke her. She was so used to being unhappy that she couldn't tell an opportunity from an obstacle.

With that mindset, she was more prone to giving up than digging in. She talked in absolutes: "always" and "never." "This always happens to me." "I never get a break."

Now, for such a black-and-white thinker, she had a surprisingly rich imagination and some serious denial running because every night she would go to bed without a plan and expect tomorrow to somehow be different from today.

When we first met, the irony of her bedtime optimism compared with her waking cynicism was completely lost on her.

I could have rearranged her entire life and schedule, but with her mindset, it would not have made a difference.

Patsy's first stop on the bullshit train was to let go of that ridiculous and sabotaging mindset. Because nothing could change until she was ready for it to.

PATRICK

Patrick's mindset was just as debilitating but shaped by too much winning—at least in his own mind. He was a decent salesman but an even smoother talker. A former jock in school with just enough success and good looks to think that life would continue to unfold for him with minimal effort because he was so talented.

Except he wasn't that talented. And talent only gets one so far. In the highly competitive world of pro sports sales, he wasn't exactly crushing his goals. He bounced around from job to job because "it just wasn't the right fit." Curiously, the only thing all those positions had in common was Patrick.

He also picked up and dropped time management tools like they were on fire. He'd give something a week and if it didn't deliver the kinds of results he wanted, he'd ditch them as fast as he adopted them.

On top of that, he was trapped in a story that had him constantly fighting everyone around him as well as himself.

His colleagues had unfair advantages over him, he was new or they had better networks or the boss was jealous or . . . blah, blah, blah. The other thing that was consistent is that it was never Patrick's fault—there was always an excellent reason why something wasn't working.

Now, it's not about blame, remember, but it definitely is about responsibility. And Patrick didn't like being held accountable for his mediocre results.

COREY

Corey works for a thriving real estate firm. He has a decent handle on his time and things are pretty good. And he's a good leader—he's often scanning the horizon for new techniques and tools to bring back to his team that will help him and everyone else get better.

When he and I first met at a conference, he had an "aha" moment during one of my presentations. He quickly recognized that by implementing one tip that I shared from the stage, his firm could quickly shave 25 to 30 percent off one of their processes and that would be a game changer.

He then asked me to provide some additional training for his company. Because he had built a culture of adaptability and curiosity, we had great buy-in from the start and, within 30 days, they had the best month in the firm's history. And that was followed by record-breaking sales for the next three months in a row.

Corey's mindset was primed for rapid adoption. He didn't need to be convinced of anything and offered little resistance to experimentation. He just needed the right tools to excel.

So . . . can you relate to any of these folks? Or do you have a completely different story running?

To find out, visit cbobbook.com/quiz and take our *Calling Bullsh*t on Busy* quiz.

THE BOTTOM LINE

There is very little magic involved in changing your relationship with time.

What's required is simply some willingness—even willingness to be willing is a great place to start.

So take the quiz to gain some clarity on where you're at and you'll be on your way. You'll find it at cbobbook.com/quiz.

I can't wait to meet you on the other side and get to work.

Chapter 1

Mindset

"Busy is the new stupid."
Warren Buffett

The most important takeaway in this entire book is that each of the following are shaping your results and success with "time management" period:

- How you think and feel about time (and, by extension, how you feel about math)
- How you talk about time (to yourself and others)
- How you act in relation to time

So if you do nothing else, bringing your full attention to these fundamental concepts and shifting your attitude and behavior will change your life.

I created the Organizational Triangle to simplify decluttering. It has three legs: One Home for Everything, Like with Like, and Something in, Something out. You can watch a short video illustrating the triangle on my YouTube channel.

In the same way that the Organizational Triangle (see page 103) simplified getting and staying organized, when you address these three concepts, you—and not the clock—will be in control of your day and therefore your life and happiness.

It is that simple—although not always easy. As the title suggests, no bullshit.

We're starting with your mindset for at least two reasons:

- If you're a type A high-achiever, you can get what you need and start using it right away.
- Like any fundamental concept, if you don't get it first, everything that comes after it may be confusing and is going to have less impact. Everything ties back to this.

So don't skip this chapter thinking your mindset is already optimized.

Time management is built on simple math. You, on the other hand, are likely a complex heap of beliefs, lies, half-formed ideas, well-meaning intentions, rumors, fantasy, and other random noise—just like most of us are. And one of those lies could be that your mindset is fine.

Any mental clutter will interfere with your ability to use the tools discussed in this book.

Also, here's the thing about tools—they're just heavy paperweights until you know how to use them correctly.

Even the best time management tool won't help if you lie or waffle or live so deeply in your own story about time that you can't use it as intended.

Here's the good news: the fundamental concepts are simple and easy to learn—you just have to be willing to learn them.

Mental clutter creates a defensive, counterproductive fog you'll need to slice through to dispel any story you're telling yourself (and anyone who will listen).

How right or wrong you are, how you know best or how you never get a break, how everyone else has it easier, how the odds are stacked against you, or how you're so broken that you're beyond hope or change . . .

All bullshit.

I get that things have happened in your life—I've had my fair share as well.

But after many years in and out of therapy and doing some deep work, it became very clear that most of the conclusions I had drawn from these events in my life were an attempt to give them meaning or reduce their impact. And to reinforce that glass-half-empty way of connecting the dots. I had become an expert at proving to myself and everyone else that the other shoe was always just about to drop.

In the end, they were just stories, not objective facts.

So if you've been rewarded emotionally when sharing your version of these stories, it just reinforces your attachment to them. There's not much incentive to let go of something that seems to be working, at least on some level.

And that's why we start with thinking and math. One is static and unchanging, and the other is likely all over the place—I'm betting you can figure out which is which.

HOW YOU THINK ABOUT TIME

What and how we think about anything shapes how we feel about that thing. As you examine your thoughts and behavior, talk about what you find using expressions like, "In the past, I would . . ." or "Historically, I did . . ." so you can draw a clear line between your choices then and now. This will help break old patterns and create a present and a future that may be informed by the past but isn't repeating the past.

NARRATIVE VS. MATH-BASED GOALS

If your historical thinking about time has been strange or messed up, it's not surprising.

That's because we measure time in quantifiable units—seconds, minutes, hours, days, and so on—and yet we set up goals using narrative, word-based outcomes typically disconnected from any unit of measurement.

So we keep score using math but run the race in words. You get that that's weird, right?

Here's what it looks like. We set up narrative goals like these:

- Work on the Smith proposal until it's finished
- Tidy the garage until it's organized
- Get so-and-so to fall in love with me

Can you see that, as stated, each of these goals has a vague, undefined end point open to interpretation?

What precisely constitutes the proposal being done? Or the garage organized? Or someone falling in love with you?

Narrative goals create confusion. Even when specific criteria for a goal is established, those criteria can change at any point. They are also susceptible to misunderstandings and misinterpretation.

Because we don't always agree on what words mean.

Narrative goals require extra time. First to define and set up the criteria and then to share them with whoever needs them to work on the task.

And it's hard to budget that extra time because there is no fixed number for how long it takes to define a goal or for everyone to fully understand the criteria.

There is potentially more wasted time if you find out that some people said they understood when they didn't.

You have none of these problems with math.

If you can count, 30 minutes means the same thing to you as it does to me.

In the past, when you worked all day on something and still didn't "finish," how did you feel?

If you felt disappointed or even demoralized, that had a direct impact on your mood, and it also influenced how you felt the next time you picked up that task or project.

Feeling crappy as a result of not getting things "done" or "done on time" means you're more likely to feel less enthusiastic and engaged on your next attempt.

And when you delegate a task with narrative goals, you're setting yourself *and* your delegate up for more work than just the task itself and similar frustrations as well.

It's very hard to budget for a process, and the successful outcome of narrative goals will be harder to assess.

All of these reasons and more are why we need to think about time in terms of math, not story.

You may not completely understand what "done" looks like, but you definitely know how long 45 minutes is.

So "work on the Smith proposal for one hour" is a lot easier to check off as completed than "finish the Smith proposal." One has a clear end point—the other does not.

Going forward, put your tasks and to-dos through the "can I measure it?" test. And when you catch yourself setting a narrative goal, call it out and switch to a math-based goal.

In Chapter 7, when we talk about planning, you'll get to see how many of your to-dos were created without a quantified finish point.

From now on, instead of saying that you're going to revise a chapter until you're finished, say, "I'm going to work on that chapter for X minutes."

Yep, it is that simple.

TIMING START-TO-FINISH TASKS

There are some tasks or errands that won't have a unit of time attached. "Buy dog food," for instance. You know it's done when you have dog food at home in the container.

But that's also because "buy dog food" is really made up of a series of smaller tasks or steps:

1. Commute to the store and park if you drove
2. Enter the store and find the dog food
3. Get in line and pay for the dog food
4. Commute home and park if you drove
5. Put the dog food in its home

Each of those steps can be timed, so even if you don't know how long something takes before you start, you will by the time you're finished. And then you can use that math to schedule the errand the next time you do it.

This means that we'll never create another task without either assigning it a math-based quantity before we start or timing it while we're doing it so we can accurately budget for it in the future.

DOING LESS IS DOING MORE

Did you ever see the plate-spinning guy on *The Ed Sullivan Show*? If not, see the endnotes for a link to this video.[2]

His act is a great visual metaphor for what busy looks like.

He'd stand a tall, skinny stick on the edge of the stage and then put a plate on top of it. He'd start spinning the stick and that would make the plate spin on top of the stick—similar to spinning a basketball on your index finger.

He'd get one plate spinning and then set up another stick, and another, until the entire apron of the stage was lined with sticks and plates spinning. Of course, as soon as he got all the way to one side of the stage, he would have to race back to the other side because those plates were starting to get wobbly.

So once every stick was up, he would run back and forth across the stage spinning each stick to keep all the plates in the air.

And this would go on for about three minutes . . . to some jazzy upbeat music.

That's your life on "busy."

You are spinning as many plates as you possibly can, except your act doesn't time out in three minutes because it isn't an act, it's your life.

So any time management system that requires you to do *more* than you're already doing is clearly not sustainable.

If you can barely keep the plates that you already have in the air spinning, how can you think that adding a few more will save you time?
And why would you? The goal is to do *less,* not *more.*

Not only should you not spin more plates, but you could probably let
a few of the current ones crash to the floor.

Because some of those plates are things you probably shouldn't have
been doing in the first place or that you've now outgrown.

YOUR 200 LIES

The average adult tells 200 lies a day.[3]

Yep, that includes you.

The good news is, you're probably not a compulsive liar.[4]

For most of us, two-thirds of those lies will never come out of our
mouths—they're just crap we tell ourselves.

You might be telling one right now if you're saying, "I *never* lie!"

Most of the lies we tell are harmless, like saying, "I'm good," when
someone asks how you are, even if you're not feeling that great.

Or when you compliment a friend on their haircut, even though you
don't love it.

That changes when you tell a colleague, "I'm so sorry to bother you,"
as you interrupt their day.

Because if you were *really* sorry to bother them, you wouldn't.

Or you'd tell the truth and say this instead: "Hey, Maya, I've got to interrupt what you're doing and give you a task that is going to take up

the rest of your day and possibly your week. I know you already have some deadlines you're working toward right now. Please let me know if you need any help prioritizing this or if anything is unclear. Thanks."

Same result, no lying.

These kinds of time-based lies come in lots of flavors. You may recognize some of these common phrases:

- "I'm so busy, I just don't have the time . . ."
- "I wish I could, but . . ."
- "I'm so sorry, but . . ."
- "I'll do it later, I promise, as soon as I . . ."
- "I'll see what I can do and get right back to you . . ."
- "That sounds great. If I only had more time, I would totally . . ."

We've got to start calling out these lies for what they are—bullshit. They are the subtle and not-so-subtle ways that we undermine our integrity and make ourselves feel bad about what we *aren't* doing.

These lies beat us down while offering false hope. We also waste precious energy and resources when we engage in fantasy instead of grounding ourselves in reality.

●— PUTTING IT INTO PRACTICE: PAYING ATTENTION

To move this from theory to practical application, start a practice of paying attention to what you say to others and especially to yourself.

Examine any excuses or explanations shared to avoid taking absolute responsibility for your behavior.

It will sting in the beginning, but it will quickly become a fun game and ultimately set you free—not to mention saving you some serious time and heartache as well.

A great place to start is every time you say "but." Usually anything you say next is a lie and undercuts whatever you said before.

A cousin of "but" is "because."

See how much time you waste coming up with a really good "because" so no one can question your reason for doing or not doing something.

To be clear, this is not a *gotcha* exercise—don't beat up on yourself when you catch yourself in one of your 200 lies. We are all guilty of them.

Just spot it, call it out, and then try to laugh rather than cry or get upset. Find the compassionate humanity in how ordinary you are instead of shaming yourself for being less than perfect.

MAKING CHOICES ABOUT YOUR TIME AND ATTENTION

You value what you choose because, by definition, it's where you've placed your attention and invested your time.

So when you choose to worry, you are valuing worry. When you choose to scroll through TikTok videos, you are valuing TikTok videos . . .

You could think, "Oh, I'm just wasting a few minutes in between appointments, no big deal," and that would mean that for those few minutes, you value wasting time.

Choosing not to choose is also a choice. You may not have considered it a choice, but it is, and it brings with it its own consequences.

What you value and where you focus your time and attention are completely up to you—the point is to make a choice.

Typically, you're more likely to get what you want when you actively choose to do or *not* do something rather than just waiting to see what happens in the vacuum of no choice.

But sometimes no choice *is* the right choice.

Sometimes waiting and seeing what develops is exactly the best choice. To get the most out of waiting and seeing, it does help to be somewhat awake and paying attention.

Not choosing because you're avoiding or ambivalent about your decision leaves your results up to chance.

The biggest problem with that choice (!) is that you may not get what you want.

Having not made a choice, you are likely to tell one of your 200 lies about your results, and how those results prove that you never get a break or always get the short end of the stick.

Both of those are bullshit—you actively abdicated all responsibility for your outcome.

Note: If you're a manager reading this book and are hoping to find a way to free up more of your team's time so you can overload them with more work than they could do before—or a manic type A person who just wants to grab *more* regardless of the emotional, psychological, and spiritual consequences of getting more—sorry. We're not playing that game.

To simply fill up your free time with more tasks, etc., is to miss one of the key points of *Calling Bullsh*t on Busy*.

We're trying to remove all the extraneous crap from your days so you have more focused moments dedicated to fewer things. That way, you can go deep and go long . . . rather than going wide and skimming across the surface.

You get more time for what is important.

What's important to you can change—importance isn't a rigidly defined thing that never shifts.

Rest could be important today, intimacy important tomorrow, and meeting a demanding deadline important before the weekend.

What you want to avoid is other people's urgent stuff flooding in and filling the vacuum created by your not choosing.

URGENT VS. IMPORTANT

Lots of people—including some of my colleagues—seem to get the concepts of "urgent" and "important" confused.

When your house is literally on fire, urgent and important are completely in sync.

You put the fire out immediately or get out of the house and then put the fire out from a safe distance—there's no mystery about what to do at that moment, right?

If your house isn't on fire—and this is almost always the case, thankfully—urgent things that are not important will try to steal your focus from what is important.

It's not urgent's fault. Urgency is loud and flashy and designed to catch your attention—like a glitzy showgirl in Vegas.

By comparison, important is steady and quiet, and easy to miss or take for granted.

So you can see why urgency often wins out when you aren't laser-focused on what's important.

And some of the 200 lies crop up when urgent is around. "I'll just get this done super quick and then get right back to X, Y, or Z . . ." Only you don't, right?

How long have you been dreaming of writing that book or going back to school, starting a family, spending more time with your family, volunteering, decluttering, or just taking a break and not feeling guilty?

And how often do you swear that you will totally do it . . . as soon as you *have the time?*

That is some serious bullshit right there because free time never just shows up.

And if you're a people pleaser, it's even worse for you. You have a permanent position on the volunteer fire department putting out everyone else's fires before getting to your own.

Look, it's nice to be nice and helpful.

It's just not so nice to constantly undermine your own success and happiness while racing around hoping everyone else sees how nice you are.

Be generous, be a team player—but if you've ever resented the time you gave away that kept you from doing something important *to you,* can you see how your choices created that situation?

When the house is not on fire, here's a simple way to tell the difference between urgent and important. Urgent by itself is almost always someone *else's* agenda.

Urgency can be a by-product of being forgetful or distracted, as in when a deadline suddenly appears for renewing your visa. But then it usually arrives with importance in tow.

When urgency shows up by itself, it's usually someone else wanting something from you on their timeline, not yours.

Get it? Urgent by itself = someone else's agenda. Urgent and important = your agenda.

KNOWING WHAT'S IMPORTANT

Given how significant knowing what's important is when making decisions, it's odd that there isn't more focus in our everyday lives on identifying what's important and why.

Fortunately, we're about to fix that. Just complete the core values exercises at cbobbook.com/values.

When you're finished, you'll have successfully identified your top 5 values. The entire set of exercises takes 25 minutes to complete.

If you've completed an exercise like this within the past year, now would be a good time to pull out your answers and see if they still apply.

If you haven't done something like this in the last 12 months, or you're thinking this sounds great but you'll do them later, or that exercises like these are a waste of time, what you're actually saying is that a fuzzy or imprecise sense of what's important to you is good enough.

But until you really know what's important to you—and I don't mean some vague sense of *sort of* knowing—you can't leverage those values to make a decision on when, where, and how you're going to invest your time.

If you tell me that your family is the most important thing to you but you've been late to one or more of your kid's events, whatever got in the way of you being on time was really what was most important to you then.

And if you're not making choices based on your values, what are you basing them on? Chance? Whimsy?

Either you're picking up a paddle or you're riding the current of life wherever it goes.

If the ride without a paddle sounds romantic or like "going with the flow," what happens when you run into rapids? Are you more likely to capsize with or without a paddle in your hands?

With the paddle, you can always coast for a while. Without the paddle, you'll never be able to steer the boat.

If you work closely with colleagues or spend time on teams or in groups, it's a great idea to do the core value exercises individually and then together as a group. Your results will help anytime you want to resolve discord in prioritizing or deciding on a direction.

Using your collective values can help remove any bias or personality conflicts when deciding between two or more competing views. They let you focus on the actual problem in front of you—deciding which choice is stronger and more aligned with your stated and agreed-upon values—not the red herring of whose idea is better.

THE WIZARD OF OZ AS A METAPHOR

The core value exercises help us bring to the conscious level what we intuitively know in our gut but may at times discount or distrust.

The movie *The Wizard of Oz* illustrates this concept beautifully.

About 25 minutes into the movie, after Dorothy and her house have been swept up in a tornado and dropped into Munchkinland, accidentally killing a wicked witch, Glinda the Good Witch shows up and tells Dorothy to take the dead witch's ruby slippers and put them on her feet. She then tells Dorothy they are very powerful and to not take them off for anything. And then she splits.

Dorothy does as she's told, but she's really just focused on finding a way back home to Kansas.

Suddenly, the dead witch's sister shows up and threatens Dorothy, and the Munchkins tell Dorothy her best bet for getting home is to follow the Yellow Brick Road and go see the Wizard of Oz.

What follows is a series of encounters—dangerous, absurd, and delightful—as Dorothy meets new friends and they all band together to find the wizard, hoping he will give them each what they think they're lacking.

Then, just when Dorothy's last chance to go home disappears, Glinda shows up again and tells her that she had the power to get back to Kansas any time she wanted—all she had to do was click her heels three times.

Now, Dorothy could have been really pissed off—that was a key piece of information that Glinda had withheld—but instead, Dorothy gives each of her new friends a big hug goodbye and clicks her way back home.

Like Dorothy, we each have our own ruby slippers—powerful, untapped knowledge of what's important and what is needed to get us to where we want to be.

We just need to consciously bring that forward and start using it when making decisions about what to focus on and when. When we marry our intuition with our core values, we consistently make better decisions with fewer regrets.

HOW YOU FEEL ABOUT TIME

Feelings may not be facts—but they can influence our behavior as if they *were* true. If in the past you felt cheated by time, or like time was out to get you, or that things took too long to do and that didn't seem fair, it wouldn't be surprising to find that you now resent time.

You may avoid being "real" with time, fearing that time will use your vulnerability against you. You may even keep secrets from time, as if time were an authority figure—even though those secrets only gaslight you.

You don't have to love time but you do need to let go of any resentments you're holding on to if you're going to maximize the time you have left. Otherwise, you'll work twice as hard.

You'll have to do what anyone would have to do to get something done *plus* try to motivate yourself, despite feeling like you've lost the battle before you even start.

Can you see how much energy is required to "act as if" when you already feel defeated?

So you don't want to pretend you don't resent time, you want to actually let yourself and time off the hook for past mistakes. You can do that by forgiving yourself—whether through prayer or meditation or expressing radical gratitude and acceptance until you feel those resentments diminish and fall away.

OVERWHELMED OR ABUNDANT

It's easy to feel overwhelmed when you're staring at a mountain of obligations.

Right now, these are the things I'm working on:

- Producing a podcast
- Writing this book
- Updating my first book, *Unstuff Your Life!,* for a new release
- Redesigning my business's website
- Creating a coaching certification program
- Delivering one of our two flagship coaching programs
- Updating the other flagship coaching program
- Developing a new enterprise time management Mastermind to coincide with the launch of this book

And I'm doing all of these things while maintaining the daily administration of my life—things like laundry, personal hygiene, working out, grocery shopping, getting enough rest, riding my bike, kayaking, socializing with friends, volunteering, meditating, sleeping, and eating.

When it's all laid out on paper it looks like a lot, right?

You may be comparing it to your list and thinking it's more than or not as much as you have to do.

Fortunately, we're not competing to see who is the busiest.

More to the point, it would certainly be a lot if I were trying to do them all at the same time, but I'm not.

And neither should you be.

If you have a lot of things to do, they will feel even more overwhelming if you pile them on top of each other and then start worrying about when you're going to do them all.

So here's the first thing you can do to simplify your list. Review it and if there is anything on it that is not aligned with your values, let it go.

If some items are there because of past choices you made that weren't aligned with your values or seemed like the "best you could do under the circumstances," you'll have to forgive yourself for those mistakes.

If you can let them go, do it. If legally or morally you have to do them, then do them as quickly as possible to settle your time (and other) debts and buy back your freedom.

If your list is filled with tasks and projects that are aligned with your personal and professional values, and if you want to do them all, just not simultaneously, then they aren't too much.

It's only your mindset that labels them as too much.

Either way, there's little point in feeling sorry for yourself or complaining—that's just wasted time.

And if you're digging yourself out of debt, time-based or otherwise, you don't have any time to waste.

On a bad day, when juggling a lot of obligations, you might view them negatively. You might start to feel trapped by the number of commitments you have.

You may even tell yourself that things are hopeless. That how you feel right now is how you'll feel forever.

That you're going to spend the rest of your life exhausted, overwhelmed, and unhappy.

Those 200 lies can be compelling, but they're not true.

Because, objectively, having more than you need (or want) is actually the definition of abundance.

So the lie says your circumstances suck. The math and the dictionary say your life is abundant. How's that for a discrepancy?

As stated, one solution for having more than you need is simple—downsize until you reach that Goldilocks state of just right, just enough.

That's when another of your 200 lies might try to convince you that letting something go will make you suffer, not set you free. Even though you might have just been complaining about all the things you had to do!

That's an all-too-real illustration of how a faulty mindset will feed you a story of "damned if you do, damned if you don't."

Can you see how powerful mindset is in influencing your thinking and feeling, and how with a faulty mindset you could make choices that do not align with your values and make things worse?

This could be boiled down to a worldview (or mindset) that is either glass half-empty or glass half-full.

Half-empty has you focused on the burden of having more than you need, the loss you'll feel if you let anything go, and viewing your life and your choices through a lens of scarcity.

Half-full sees that not only do you have everything you need, but you have more than you need. That you are in a state of abundance—which is something to celebrate and be grateful for.

You are living in a state of plenty, not lack—if you are willing to see it that way.

But those 200 lies, fueled by your ego, will fight hard to persuade you otherwise.

Now, there may be parts of a project or a task that you don't enjoy doing.

You might not want to do all the stuff on your to-do list.

You don't have to.

Delegate them to someone else, automate them, or decide they don't need to be done by anyone and cross them off.

You are in control of what gets done when and by whom.

And when you use your values to make decisions, you shift from deciding if a task is "bad" or "good" to deciding if the task is worth your time and energy or not.

In fact, whether we're talking about clutter or tasks, your sense of what's good or bad comes down to how you feel about it in the moment more than objective truth.

Which is brilliantly illustrated in the Taoist parable "Maybe."

A poor farmer's horse runs off. That night, his neighbors gather around to mourn his loss. "We cannot believe this. What a terrible thing has happened to you," they say. And the farmer responds, "Maybe."

Days later, the farmer's horse returns with seven wild horses in tow. Right away, the neighbors exclaim, "What unexpected good fortune!" The farmer shrugs. "Maybe."

The next day, the farmer's son rides one of the wild horses, falls off, and breaks his leg. The neighbors cry, "What terrible fortune has befallen your son!" The farmer replies, "Maybe."

A few weeks later, the army comes through the village drafting men for the war. When they see the farmer's son and his broken leg, they pass him by. The neighbors rejoice. "What great luck for you and your son!" The farmer simply says, "Maybe."

Value, like beauty, is in the eye of the beholder.

GRATITUDE AS A CURE FOR OVERWHELM

Rather than riding the seesaw of good and bad up and down, why not set any judgments aside and shift how you feel about time and commitments instead?

Instead of thinking, "I have way too much to do," and feeling crappy about it, try thinking, "Too much is better than too little," and foster a sense of gratitude.

Then continue building on that gratitude by focusing on a larger, macro view of your life.

Swap dwelling on whether any one task or project delights you in the moment with celebrating that you are actively curating your day—and, by extension, your life, every day.

You are not a puppet or a doll being manipulated into doing anything. You have the intelligence to decide what is important to you and the agency to act on that decision. That is a great position to be in and something to honor and protect—it's not a burden or an imposition.

There are many people in the world right now whose circumstances are far more grim. You don't need to feel guilty about that, but you also shouldn't take your relative comfort for granted.

Starting there, it becomes much easier to appreciate everything that is present in your life.

Something else I've discovered over the past 26+ years: fighting with stuff or time doesn't work.

When it comes to clutter, you have to physically move it—you won't think your way to an organized home.

And when it comes to time, resisting the 24-hour system and the steady flow of time won't change that system one bit. Seriously.

So another mindset shift could be away from resenting time and the tasks you have to do and toward embracing and doing them, or delegating or ditching them.

The neuroscience behind this tells us that people who express and feel gratitude have a higher volume of gray matter in their brains, which enables us to better control our movements, memories, and emotions. Focusing on gratitude enhances dopamine and serotonin, the neurotransmitters of happiness.[5]

●— PUTTING IT INTO PRACTICE: GRATITUDE

Here's a quick way to jump-start your gratitude practice. Turn to whatever is kicking your butt in this moment, whether that is clutter or too many chores, and say, "Thank you for being in my life. You served me at one time and you no longer do. I now release you."

You will instantly feel different. The grasp that clutter or some task was holding you in will loosen. You may have to say the phrase a few times for the grip to fall away completely, but with repetition it will.

Gratitude lists are another easy way to turn up the volume on what's present and going well in your life. I start each day with a simple list of at least five specific things I'm grateful for. So instead of saying I'm grateful for my health (general), I say I'm grateful for the flexibility to bend over and tie my shoes without lower back pain (specific).

As I fall asleep each night, I also run through a list of all the people and experiences I am grateful for that day. I am consistently asleep before the list is finished.

We'll talk about triage in Chapter 7, Poor Planning—for now, just recognize that as long as you are alive, there will always be more things to do than there is time to do them. You're not trying to get to the task version of Inbox Zero.

When you start to employ this mindset shift and any of these habits, you will feel better about the work you're doing, the stress and tension you're feeling will soften and break apart quicker, and life will feel easier.

Believe it or not, your attitude and consistency are far more important to your success or failure than your ability to be disciplined.[6]

Spending 5 to 15 minutes a day doing something consistently is the time management version of compound interest—it yields higher returns for the same amount of time invested.

Think back to any term paper or report. When you crammed, you may have met the deadline, but you got there just in time and exhausted. There was no time for any revisions to make the paper better. Had you budgeted the same amount of time over a few weeks, you would have been able to update the paper until you were satisfied and still had time to take breaks.

COMFORT VS. VALUES

I think the world looks the way it does today—greater polarization, rising temperatures, dwindling resources—because we as a society have made a lot of shitty choices focused on short-term gain.

The people in power have pushed off responsibility for and thoughtful stewardship of our shared planet onto some undefined future generation—a macro version of "buy now, pay later" and the "deferred decisions" that create clutter.

On the micro side, that is enabled by many of us in the West, and in the US in particular, who maintain an almost absurd attachment to our relative comfort in the moment, often to the detriment of our long-term goals.

If your basic needs aren't being met, comfort is important, and one result of a bigger structural problem that this book isn't equipped to solve. No one should be hungry or unsheltered unless they have actively chosen to be.

For the rest of us, comfort is a fool's errand, because we're *already* comfortable. If you're reading this book, you very likely have a roof over your head, food in your belly, and clean clothes on your back.

So, practically speaking, something that pushes you outside your comfort zone is probably still not pushing you that far.

If your first reaction to that is "But I like my comfort," the cure for overvaluing your comfort is not to become permanently miserable. There are miles between those two polar opposites.

Just consider this an invitation to focus more on becoming your biggest, baddest, best self and less on how that feels at every moment.

What fires you up, what gets your engine stoked? What inspires you to push forward regardless of headwinds or resistance?

To rise to that level, you've got to be clear about what is important to you. And you're going to have to exert yourself—which might not be comfortable.

If you've resisted staking a claim for what actually matters to you because asserting yourself has been uncomfortable, let's swap that discomfort for this discomfort. If you're going to be uncomfortable, you might as well have something awesome to show for it.

And if you are currently crushing your goals and living an amazing life, you already have a certain tolerance for discomfort. You are perfectly set up to use this book to optimize your time even more.

A world where everyone is engaged and lit up, bursting with life force and energy—where we're primarily focused on activities, experiences, and relationships that move our hearts and feed our minds and spirits—is a rich, robust, and diverse world.

It's the kind of world I think most of us want to live in.

To get there, we're each going to have to be willing to be momentarily uncomfortable at times.

That doesn't mean a life of misery and drudgery—that's so dramatic!

It just means that choosing activities aligned with your values may sometimes be uncomfortable. Not naked-and-hungry-and-cold-forever uncomfortable. Just temporarily uncomfortable.

You'll swap superficial comfort while being secretly miserable at your core for a little temporary discomfort while being overwhelmingly satisfied and happy at your core.

Which discomfort is more insidious—the one that tells you sweat, effort, and challenges are to be avoided at all costs *or* the one that hums constantly in the background, spoiling any sense of satisfaction?

You'll forget the first kind in 24 hours or less. The second kind will actively prevent everything you dream of and are capable of from ever happening.

HOW YOU INTERACT WITH TIME

How you think and feel about time directly impacts your actions—whether you're enthusiastic and digging in or disinterested and tentative.

You can do anything, in spite of how you're feeling—it will just take a lot of energy or require you to jump into action before thinking and feeling.

You can definitely change how you think and feel through physical activity. *Move a muscle, change a thought* or *Move a muscle, change a feeling.*

It's just that, for most of us, we want to *feel* like getting up and moving before we get up and move. So if we're not feeling it yet, we're stuck in a Catch-22 situation. We need to move to shift our feelings but we don't feel like moving so we stay where we are.

Ultimately, regardless of what you think or how you feel, actions speak the loudest when it comes to time management.

If you half-ass your efforts, or do the wrong thing at the right time, or even the right thing at the wrong time, you're likely to get sub-par results. Even if you do the right thing at the right time, you might not see exceptional results. A faulty mindset and wobbly feelings will use these results to "prove" that time always has the upper hand and you can't win.

Bullshit. Improving time management is an objective game of trial-and-error—you've got to be willing to keep trying regardless of your immediate results. Simon Sinek brilliantly illustrates this point—see the endnotes to watch a video of him explaining it.[7]

GOLF BALLS, PEBBLES, AND SAND

What's up with the story that says, "Let's get a bunch of small, unimportant tasks out of the way so we can open up a block of time with no distractions for that big sexy project"?

I have fallen for that lie more than once myself.

And every time I burn through the day knocking out a bunch of inconsequential crap, by the time I'm ready to take on the big work, I'm exhausted.

Then I tell myself another one of my 200 lies—tomorrow will be different. I'll get up early and do the big thing then.

Sound familiar?

In reality, it's completely backward.

First off, those little tasks often take longer than expected.

And then, like a demonic game of Whac-A-Mole, another task always pops up demanding attention.

Even if you're nodding your head right now, it may still be hard to accept that small things first is not the way to go—and here's why.

First, there's the dopamine hit you get when you check something off your list, even something small and insignificant.

Then one of your 200 lies might tell you that there aren't that many of them and that you'll get them done faster than you think.

The lie may even tell you that you are the exception to this rule, or that you're clever enough that the rule doesn't apply to you. But there is a video that illustrates this point simply and clearly.

In the video, a professor shows his class how hard it is to fit the big things into your life when you start by focusing on the small stuff. He does this with golf balls representing the "big" stuff and sand as the "small" stuff. Filling a jar with sand first leaves no room for the golf balls. When he puts the golf balls in first, the sand easily flows around the balls and everything seems to fit.[8]

Lots of people focus on the small stuff, thinking the big stuff can wait and that they'll definitely get to it soon, or one day, or someday.

But time and life don't work that way.

And I understand it can feel counterintuitive—that getting all the busywork out of the way *should* leave time for all the big things.

But that is exactly how we nickel-and-dime ourselves out of an entire year of our lives. And it happens in 5- and 10-minute increments.

Remember Patsy from the previous chapter?

Patsy was always rushing around dealing with whatever was urgent. A phone call, text message, email, doorbell, errand, chore—it didn't matter.

She was so busy that she couldn't even tell if she was having a good day or a bad day until it was over. And then pretty much every day ended badly. She was constantly *reacting* to the world around her, rather than *acting* on her own terms.

And when she got a completely free day, she had no idea what to do with it.

She'd surf the internet, scroll through social media, play some solitaire, and watch the clock. She'd tell herself she was relaxing but really she was just waiting for the day to end so she could get back to a routine she understood—racing through tasks at breakneck speed, then crashing at the end of the day, exhausted.

We typically choose the devil we know even when he's trouble.

Fortunately, after a few weeks of us working together, Patsy started to shift her mindset.

She used the tools outlined in this book—a timer, a stopwatch, and a calendar. She did the core value exercises, began writing a daily gratitude list, slowly broke free from her old way of thinking, and started making progress.

When we're in overload, like Patsy, getting *any* relief sometimes feels like a good strategy.

We consider what's required to move a golf ball, and the sand looks much more appealing.

We don't think about the satisfaction we'll get after tackling one of our golf balls—that seems too abstract and far away. And unfortunately, there's always more sand.

WHO ARE YOUR ROLE MODELS?
You might be thinking, "Well, okay, Patsy was a mess. What about Oprah or Bill Gates—they get lots done every day!"

They do, and most billionaires have staff.

Of course, they weren't always billionaires, but I'll bet they both knew the difference between the golf balls and the sand and were almost maniacal about shutting out anything that might have been standing between them and their goals.

So if you're willing to match their focus and attack your life with that much intensity, they could be great role models.

It's just that most people really like their comfort.

There are plenty of stories about the early days at Microsoft that say when Gates was programming, he would often pull all-nighters, sometimes many in a row. It seems he regularly worked 80 to 120 hours a week, to the exclusion of most other things.

Are you willing to do that? Are you able to do that? If not, what can you afford to do—or not do?

Ultimately, modeling your life on anyone else isn't that helpful.

You are you, with your own set of circumstances—so let's hack your life and get you as much time as we can for the things you think are most important.

THE BOTTOM LINE

You can't change your relationship to time without changing how you think, feel, and interact with it. That's why *Calling Bullsh*t on Busy* starts with mindset.

It's the fundamental stepping stone to everything that comes after.

The best tools in the world are just paperweights if you don't know how to use them, so don't underestimate or neglect shifting your mindset if you want to change your approach to time.

CHAPTER RECAP

To get control over your day and your life, you're going to need to change your relationship with time. That requires changing three things at a fundamental level:

- How you think about time
- How you feel about time
- How you interact with time

HOW YOU THINK ABOUT TIME

In the past, you may have thought that time was slippery and hard to pin down. Sometimes it raced by, other times it dragged on.

Stories about how you use time may be slanted to prove you are losing the war with time, particularly if you've got a glass-half-empty mindset.

To interrupt those stories or set them aside, stop trying to evaluate your relationship with time. Instead, focus on how you measure time: 60 seconds in a minute, 60 minutes in an hour, 24 hours in a day.

Then shift from stating narrative goals like working on something until you're "done" to using math-based goals, like working on something for X minutes.

You'll get more done and feel more accomplished when you swap "cleaning the garage" for "cleaning the garage for 30 minutes," and then set a timer. When the timer goes off, if you actually worked in the garage for all 30 minutes, you did what you said you were going to do. You win.

Getting time back so you can do more means doing less or, more specifically, doing fewer things but doing them deeper and more thoroughly. Productivity isn't necessarily about keeping more plates spinning. It's about committing to what matters most to you and using those values to decide which plates need to stay in the air and which can now crash to the floor without negatively impacting your life.

Math doesn't lie, but humans do. The average adult tells 200 lies per day—mostly to themselves. Start paying attention to the false stories that rob you of time. Stories like "I'm a hopeless procrastinator" or "I never catch a break." These kinds of falsehoods do not serve you. You don't get a pass because you're so "bad at time." Get better at how you use your time and you'll see that these stories have been holding you back and defining your reality. When you let these lies go, you will quickly find that you have the same amount of time as everyone else.

Back to values. By definition, what you choose is what you value. It is the clearest demonstration of where you've invested your time and attention. Make sure to prioritize the important over the urgent when-ever possible. Sometimes what's urgent will demand your attention, and if it's both urgent and important, it deserves your attention, like when something is literally on fire.

But often urgent will just be jumping up and down, trying to get your attention regardless of its significance. With some practice, you can learn to ignore that insistence and stay focused on what's actually important, regardless of its urgency.

If you're struggling to figure out if something is both urgent and important, it's probably not both. A simple thumbnail to help you distinguish urgent from important is this: Urgent by itself = someone else's agenda. Important = your agenda.

To nail down exactly what is important to you, complete the core value exercises at cbobbook.com/values. When you're finished (in about 25 minutes), you'll have identified your top 5 values and can then use them to further identify what is worthy of your time and attention and what you can let go of.

Until you know what's important to you and then leverage those values every time you decide how, when, and where to invest your time, you may never "get around" to the things that matter. You may continue to tell yourself that there is something you need to "get out of the way" first so you have "enough" time to focus on what's important. Hopefully, you can now start to see that that is the exact opposite of how you should be approaching what matters most.

HOW YOU FEEL ABOUT TIME

Feelings aren't facts, but they can influence our choices around time, consciously and unconsciously. Feelings are the basis for many of those stories in which you are running late, are running out of time, or end up losing the battle with time.

Gratitude is an instant cure for feeling overwhelmed. "Too much to do" can be seen (and felt) as an abundance of opportunities just as easily as it can be seen as a relentless, unyielding burden. So flip the script on feeling bothered by all that abundance and take a moment to celebrate the fact that you have so much going on in the first place.

Turn to whatever it is that is kicking your butt in the moment, whether that is too much stuff (clutter) or too many chores, and say, "Thank you for being present in my life. You served me at one time and you no longer do. I now release you." It will instantly improve your mood and your results.

Consider starting a practice, if you don't already have one, of writing simple gratitude lists when you wake up and at the end of your day to stay positive about what is present in your life rather than focusing on what is missing. Be specific when you call out what you are grateful for. Instead of just being grateful for your health, what *about* your health are you grateful for—flexibility to bend over without pain, shedding X pounds, a clean cancer screening?

Embrace or at least accept that some short-term discomfort may be required to get you long-term success. If you are more comfortable than you typically consider or acknowledge—you're not lacking food, clothing, or shelter—you don't have to resign yourself to a life of misery to make progress. You just have to be willing to sit in temporary discomfort every now and then. Few if any significant things ever happen in the middle of someone's "comfort zone."

HOW YOU INTERACT WITH TIME

Once you've addressed how you think and feel about time, you'll want to get into action, and you'll want to do that with clarity and decisiveness.

Like any skill, the more you practice using your time deliberately, the better at it you'll become.

With the proper mindset, you'll be able to quiet down those 200 lies that tell you either that you have all the time in the world or that you have so little time available that you will never catch up. From there, you can start to prioritize what's important to you and what is aligned with your current core values.

BIG THINGS FIRST

There is a pervasive myth that getting a bunch of small, unimportant tasks out of the way first will open up a big block of unstructured time so you can then do your big work. But once you've burned through your time with busywork, you're often too tired to dig into that big work, right?

So, like a lot of other people, you may end up pushing the big stuff off, telling yourself that you will definitely get to it soon, or one day, or, worse, someday. And before you know it, you'll have nickel-and-dimed yourself out of a year or more of your life—in 5- and 10-minute increments.

Professor Meir Kay illustrates this in a simple video you'll find in End Note 8. Using golf balls to represent the "big" stuff and sand as the "small" stuff, he fills a jar up with sand. Not surprisingly, there is no room left in the jar for any golf balls.

When he puts the golf balls in first, the sand easily flows around the balls and everything seems to fit.

So even though it may feel counterintuitive, develop the practice of prioritizing the big things, your golf balls, first. You'll get the little things done, too . . . or even better, you'll delegate them away or decide they don't need to be done at all.

Chapter 2
Tools

"It's not the load that breaks you down;
it's the way you carry it."
Lena Horne

Whenever I'm teaching a group of people, in person or online, we start the same way. I share our agenda for the session and then we take three deep breaths together.

So even though you and I aren't in the same room and we aren't taking those breaths at the exact same time, let's start by having you take three deep breaths.

You might think it silly since I can't see you doing it.

Except you're not doing it for me . . . You're doing it for you.

If you're rolling your eyes right now, I'm reminded of what Marianne Williamson said one night when she was coaching a group of us at the Saban Theater, "Cynical and aloof—how's that working for you?"

If you're in a public place and feeling self-conscious, you're already breathing, right? No one is watching you that closely or even cares.

And if taking three deep, focused breaths will likely get you what you want faster and with less effort, why would you hesitate for a second?

So your resistance becomes a teachable moment. When resistance occurs, it's almost always worth examining.

Consider how often you undermine your own success because you're more concerned with how you look to others than with how you feel in the moment.

Not every suggestion in this book may be useful to you—but if you're unwilling to at least experiment with each of them, you'll never find out for sure.

I've found that maintaining a sense of curiosity rather than resistance has consistently brought better results, even when I might consider the experiment a failure.

THREE BREATHS AND STRESS

Brain science tells us that the central nervous system can be reset in as few as three deep breaths.[9]

So I'm not suggesting that you do them because they connect you to source energy or raise your vibration or magically align your third chakra. They might . . . but let's focus on the practical for now.

The science tells us that they'll calm you down and help you focus. And they take less than 30 seconds to complete.

So anytime you're having a shitty day or a shitty moment and you want to wipe the slate clean and start over, you can. With three deep breaths.

Look, you just got your first tool and exposed some possible unconscious bias. Not a bad start, eh?

Wherever you are right now, physically and mentally, you're probably familiar with that heart-racing, hands-shaking kind of stress response. Fight or flight. That's when your body feels like it's about to run for its life or do battle with a Goliath-sized opponent.

For most of us, Goliath is—thankfully—almost never a physical foe, so you can tuck your slingshot back in your pocket for another day.

Much more often it's a tough conversation with a client, a looming work deadline, or some other dreaded event where the outcome is uncertain.

And part of that fear is because we're scared we're about to get something we don't want (judgment, rejection, scolding, or some other blow to our ego) or lose something we don't want to give up.

Whenever anything disturbing happens, in the outside world or inside your mind, modulating your breath is a simple and reliable way to regulate your response to stress.

YOU CONTROL THE STORY OR IT CONTROLS YOU

Whatever's going on in your life, chances are you've got a story about it. Our brains *love* stories, although I tend to refer to stories as just "story."

Story is one of the primary ways we process information and context. For humans, story is boss.

So even if you're perfectly safe right now, throughout the day thoughts may arise where you relive the fight you recently had with your partner, or you start fretting over a presentation for work tomorrow—all of which will flip you or, more specifically, your body into fight-or-flight mode.

The word we often use to describe this state is "stress," and all of us know what it feels like.

Some stress is good; it doesn't negatively impact us.[10] The stress I'm talking about here, though, is the stress we don't want.

People often end up in one of our programs because of stress.

They're anxious or depressed, not sleeping, or experiencing some other form of chronic stress. They're drowning in clutter, or they can't seem to stop procrastinating, or they're fighting with the people they love over *stuff* and they're desperate for something to fix it, and the quicker the better.

And the path to that relief starts with three deep breaths.

It's something you can do anytime, anywhere. It can't magically solve all your problems, but it will reset your nervous system and put your body in a more relaxed, calmer state. Almost instantly.[11]

Deep breathing puts the brakes on that full-body stress response that leaves us shaky, anxious, and overwhelmed.

BREATHING QUIETS THE MIND

Three breaths can make us calmer, more relaxed, and feeling just a tiny bit more in control. It changes the voice in our heads from "Holy shit, what is going on here?" to "It's going to be okay. Just take one step at a time. You've got this, pal."

Which, as it turns out, is a much better frame of mind for getting things done. Spinning out with that first voice is bad for your productivity.

And if you're telling yourself you don't have time to take three deep breaths, that is definitely one of your 200 lies—you're already breathing.

So, wherever you are, even if your inner voice is telling you that focused breathing is stupid and pointless, try it anyway.

●— PUTTING IT INTO PRACTICE: THREE DEEP BREATHS

To get started, shake out your muscles, get comfortable, and take three deep breaths—the deeper, the better. Breathe in through your nose until you can't take in any more air, and then take another sip or two if you can. Hold it for a second. Then slowly breathe out through your mouth. Exhale all the air in your lungs, and then keep breathing out just a little bit more.

See if you can take each breath over a count of five seconds, both on the way in and out. And if you can hold your breath between inhaling and exhaling for a count of one or two, even better.

You can count using the Mississippi method, as in "One Mississippi. Two Mississippi. Three Mississippi. Four Mississippi. Five Mississippi." Then back out again for the same number of Mississippis.

On the whole, modern humans are lazy breathers. We take shallow breaths that leave our brains low on oxygen.

Keep this exercise with you. Use it to reset your brain when you need to, whether you're transitioning from work time to family time, or preparing for a big presentation.

I can't stress enough what a powerful tool the breath is, and it comes factory-installed. If you are alive as you read these words, you're already doing it—you just want to bring your awareness to it more completely.

SETTING INTENTIONS

And now that you're grounded and poised for success, set a timer for 15 seconds—or 30 seconds if that feels better.

Then, while the timer is running, set an intention for yourself. What do you want to take away from this book or what would you like to let go of by reading this book?

Ask yourself the question, and see what comes up.

Once you've settled on your intention, *write it down*.

We'll revisit a few themes again and again in this book, and putting things in writing is one of them. If you don't write things down, you'll forget what they were, and you'll have no easy way of getting them back or checking them off your list.

So give yourself the quick win of experiencing some progress—free dopamine hit!—and start writing stuff down.

This ties into a larger concept of "You can't manage what you don't measure."

You'll be amazed at how much you can get done when you record your intentions and then measure your progress toward manifesting them.[12]

If you want to join others reading this book and get some extra support and momentum, go to facebook.com/cbobbook and share your intention with us there.

FYI, if your reaction to this exercise is similar to your reaction to the breathing, consider this: contempt prior to investigation is a surefire way to double down on what you already know and believe. And it's guaranteed to shut you off from any solution you didn't think up yourself.

Instead of trying to convince you to keep an open mind, I'll just ask you to be honest with yourself about how successful your current methods are and what it is you think you'll lose by trying something else.

You can always return to your old way of doing things if these suggestions don't deliver results.

When you want to focus your mind and energy and make something specific happen quickly, set an intention.

THREE TIME MANAGEMENT TOOLS

THE TIMER

Let's talk about the second-most important tool in your time management toolbox first—a timer.

In the previous chapter, we talked about the importance of quantifying objectives, and this is the tool you're going to use to shift from narrative goals to math-based goals.

No more working on a task until it's "finished," since that is too open to interpretation and uncertainty. Now you're going to pick an amount of time to work on something and set your timer.

If you want to take this up a notch, declare the amount of time out loud, either to yourself or to an accountability partner. Either way, when the timer goes off, the task is complete.

If there's time in your schedule and you want to continue working on the same task, set the timer for another quantity of time—it doesn't have to be the same duration as last time.

Ideally, work in 15-minute increments, with 15 minutes being the minimum, and three-hour blocks of time being the very most.

It's hard to stay focused on a single task for more than about three hours without getting punchy.[13]

Some suggest up to four hours, but why push it?[14]

So shift gears every three hours or so, even when you're laboring away at a tight deadline.

When I wrote this book, I did it in one- and two-hour blocks of time.

I'd set the timer and when it went off, I'd highlight the text on the page in red so I could find my place easily, then get up and move my body and drink some water. Then I'd come back to my desk and set the timer for another chunk of time.

Note to those with ADHD or other attention challenges: You might be saying, "But, Andrew, this whole 'time segment' thing freaks me out. I can't stay focused for more than five minutes at a time. Help!"

If 15 minutes is too long, adjust the blocks of time down until you find your sweet spot. Using the second tool, a stopwatch, measure how long you can work uninterrupted before you lose focus.

If it's five minutes, great. If it's three minutes, that's fine, too.

The length of time isn't as important as using a timer to establish duration.

So, whether it's three minutes or three hours, success is measured by working uninterrupted until the timer goes off.

We know that when we're working toward a goal and that goal is hard to nail down—i.e., "finished,"—and then we don't achieve it, that failure influences how we feel going forward.

In the moment, it might kick up some of your 200 lies about how difficult the task was and how slippery the goal was, too.

You may even toss in a few zingers about how much you suck at other things while you're at it. Objectively, it's amazing the kind of crap we'll direct at ourselves sometimes.

And then, if you're optimistic (or foolish) enough to try it again, before you even begin, you've got a story going about how poorly you did last time and you're worrying that this time will be the same or even worse.

It often doesn't make a lot of sense, but then our feelings aren't always logical.

This is a perfect example of failure breeding failure.

Conversely, with a timer, staying focused is the task, nothing else. When the timer dings and you remained focused, you were successful. And success breeds success.

That feeling of success, while not as powerful as the feeling of failure,[15] builds on itself so that the next time you set the timer, you're feeling optimistic and enthusiastic about staying focused for the duration.

THE STOPWATCH
The timer determines when you'll stop working on something without interruptions.

You'll use the stopwatch to figure out how long it takes to do something that has to be completed in one block of time, like commute to the office.

You can't really set a timer and say you'll stop commuting at 30 minutes when the timer goes off, right? What if you're only halfway there?

And when you guesstimate, if you're like most people, you're either under- or overestimating how long things take.[16]

So let's accurately find out how long it takes to commute to work, do laundry, and shop for groceries, so you can book enough time on your calendar.

Over the next seven days, time yourself doing each recurring task and write your results down. That should include getting yourself ready in the morning, getting the kids ready if you have kids, making meals, running errands, etc.

If you do it more than once a year, time it.

When you've captured three different instances of a repeated task, especially any that involve driving, average those results together and use that as your basis for scheduling.

We also talk about this as a "noble experiment" in Chapter 7.

This exercise can be a bit intrusive and annoying, I know. When you see how long some things take and how quickly others get done, the gap between your imagination and reality may shock you and even piss you off.

But it's an invaluable exercise and you will be blown away by what you discover.

You'll learn what you do well and quickly, and what you don't do well or quickly, regardless of how much you enjoy doing it.

In my case, I really enjoy doing the laundry, even though I don't do it that fast. So I do it on a day when I'm working from home, where the pacing doesn't impact anything else.

In addition to correctly budgeting enough time on your calendar, you can use the info you gather to make conscious choices about what you want to do and what that task will cost you.

In this system that isn't a system, you're allowed to do things that take a long time or that you don't do particularly well but enjoy doing.

As long as you are conscious of the choice you're making and all of its costs—time, money, etc.—you can do whatever you want. Because your time is your own and your happiness matters.

The goal is not to become an unhappy tasking robot just because you discovered the most efficient choice.

If you want to do something, do it. Just don't lie to yourself about it or complain later about not having enough time to do something else.

It's like buying something you can't really afford but tell yourself you've got to have.

You could call it an investment or another of your 200 lies to convince yourself that there's a good or legitimate reason for the purchase.

But ultimately it comes down to wanting what you want when you want it. The end of that sentence often just leaves off "and I'm willing to pay the price without lying about the consequences."

THE CALENDAR

All of the data gathering involving the stopwatch and timer is necessary so you can effectively schedule both recurring and one-off tasks on your calendar, the third time management power tool.

The calendar is how you drive your day and is essential to your success.

What kind of calendar you use—paper or digital—is up to you. The only downsides to a paper calendar are carrying it around with you and making corrections or updates. If you are often moving appointments around, a paper calendar may start to look messy or be filled with correction tape. If you don't mind, I don't either.

I use a digital calendar because it's more flexible and it's free—I don't have to buy a new one every year. It syncs across both of my devices so I can access the same information on my laptop and my smartphone. It also gives my assistant access to the same information, since she sets many external appointments for me.

Changing an appointment is as easy as dragging and dropping it wherever it needs to go.

In the old days, when I used the Franklin Planner, I had to erase or white out any updates to the calendar.

If you're curious about migrating to a digital calendar from a paper calendar, you can experiment with Google's calendar, the calendar inside Microsoft's Outlook, the calendar bundled into Apple's OS, or any number of free apps. You can also see what my calendar looks like at cbobbook.com/tools.

And if you like paper, stick with what you like. Just factor in that using a paper calendar will cost you some money—buying a new one each year, correction tape, pens—and also some time when you manually update any changes to your schedule. It also requires you to be a bit more organized, since you'll always want to have your calendar with you.

Do what serves you and brings you happiness—just don't then complain about it.

If you're complaining about something, you're wasting time the second time you open your mouth. The first time is part of the process of discovering you're unhappy and articulating it. The minutes spent complaining about it more than once is time you could redirect into finding a better solution.

TO-DO LISTS

A to-do list is not a time management tool—it's a way to get everything out of your head and in one location so nothing gets missed or forgotten.

We'll go deeper into to-do lists in Chapter 7, when we look at planning. For now, you just need to know that your list is a container, not a plan.

The things on your to-do list won't get done until you pick a specific date and time to do them. Which is what makes the calendar your foundational tool.

Your calendar is your road map for what you will do on any given day, and for how long.

When you start living by your calendar instead of a bunch of Post-its or notes scribbled on the back of an envelope or relying on your memory, you will take a major step forward in reclaiming your time and your life.

Because if it's not on your calendar, you haven't committed to it yet. It's easy to say, "I'll get to that in a bit" or "I will definitely do that later," and think you mean it when you say it.

By the way, there are two kinds of "later." There's the later you mean when you say, "I will do that later, at 4:00 p.m. on Saturday." That's a real later.

The other later is the stepchild of "someday," and it will never arrive. That's the one that sounds like this: "I'm totally slammed right now and I'm going to have to deal with that later."

When you say you'll do a thing "someday," you are more often than not telling one of your 200 lies, because "someday" isn't a day on any calendar. And as we've already discussed, if it isn't on your calendar, it's not going to happen.

Keep your ears open for how often you use "later" or "someday" and what you can do to either commit to a date and time or let the activity go.

Building the habit of scheduling things you want to do on specific dates and at specific times helps ensure they happen.

TIME BUCKETS

Another problem with to-do lists is that they often end up all over the place and with everything on them.

If you've only got one list, "Pick up the dry cleaning" could be listed before "Make a doctor's appointment" and "Help the kids with their science project," regardless of which is more important.

Other times, you keep writing the same things over and over again because you don't want to forget them and because you can't find your previous lists.

So, as a container, lists aren't the best tool. That's where time buckets come in.

Regardless of how anyone else may define time buckets, I use the term to refer to a three-dimensional and inclusive way of assigning and grouping similar tasks together. Rather than just slapping a category on tasks and trying to arrange them vertically, I prefer to group them together and drop them into a bucket—then prioritize inside the bucket.

It's the second leg of the Organizational Triangle, Like with Like, for time.

If you're a visual person like me, time buckets help you see similar tasks as you're sorting them. Another bonus is that even a huge bucket has a finite amount of space. They'll eventually fill up, so you've got to be conscious of what and how much you put in them.

You can see my time buckets and download a starter set of your own at cbobbook.com/tools.

You'll want to make your buckets specific enough to separate tasks from each other easily, but not so hyperspecific that you end up with a bunch of one-task buckets.

If you've struggled with how to prioritize tasks in the past, this method of sorting should help you.

With only one to-do list, you'll eventually end up with two or more high-priority tasks competing for first place, which can be an impossible choice to make.

Getting a worrisome mole checked out shouldn't be pitted against finishing up a major report for work, right? They're both important. If you had a Work bucket and a Health & Medical bucket, they could each be in first place in their own buckets.

You'll learn more about using time buckets to prioritize your tasks in Chapter 7.

THE PARETO PRINCIPLE (OR THE 80/20 RULE)

Have you heard of the Pareto Principle? You may know it as the 80/20 rule. If not, it's about to change your life.

The Pareto Principle was named for a 19th-century Italian economist, Vilfredo Pareto, who discovered something curious: 80 percent of the land in Italy was owned by 20 percent of the population.

Even more curious, he started to see this 80/20 split play itself out in lots of other ways. For example, 80 percent of a company's income often comes from 20 percent of its best clients.

And, in the context of your life, you can use the Pareto Principle to help you prioritize, too.

What if you figured out which 20 percent of your efforts delivered the biggest and best results? Imagine what would happen if you doubled the 20 percent of the time you spend on those activities?

You'll get to see how powerful this can be in Chapter 7.

A FEW OTHER TIME STATS

The average person is interrupted by communications technology every 10 minutes. For every interruption, it takes our brains up to 25 minutes to recover and refocus on what we were doing.

That means that two interruptions and two recoveries could equal up to one hour lost. But it gets worse.

In that hour, you might have been interrupted three more times.

With that many interruptions each hour, you haven't even fully recovered before you're interrupted again.

If you saw that in a slapstick comedy you might find it amusing. Picture it. Someone gets knocked down. They fumble around, trying to get their bearings. They wobble and try to get back on their feet. They are clawing their way upright and then they get knocked down again. Funny in a movie—in your life, not so much.

Is it any surprise that so many of us get to the end of a hectic day and feel like we've been through the wringer, because we have, and we have nothing to show for it?

Actually, we have plenty to show for it in the form of exhaustion, frustration, and more to do than when we started the day . . . but we've accomplished very little or nothing that actually matters.

That's the kind of busy we need to call bullshit on now.

HIGH-VALUE ACTIVITIES

When you're that kind of busy, you end up pushing the most important tasks—your golf balls—to the back burner again. So whether you're delaying them until you have some unstructured time or avoiding them because you don't have the energy or concentration to give them the attention they need, that's a problem.

One way to turn this around and take action quickly is to chunk your golf balls up into bite-sized HVAs (high-value activities) and do just three of them before the day gets away from you. By design, HVAs are intended to be short and quick.

I first learned of this idea from a friend and mentor, speaker and author Mark LeBlanc. He teaches people to identify and then act on three HVAs every day to grow their businesses.

Let's expand the definition of HVAs to include any quick, finite action you can take in your professional *or* personal life. They could be quick work tasks, like the following:

- Call a prospect
- Email or call an old connection
- Send a card or a mailer to reconnect with a lead
- Make or reach out to one new contact

Or they could be more intimate personal activities:

- Do 10 burpees or pushups
- Make your bed
- Write down 10 things you're grateful for
- Send a surprise voicemail or text message to a loved one

Or they could be a combination of work and life activities. You might have different HVAs on work days than on weekends and whether you're home or on vacation. The idea is to do a few quick things first thing in the morning that are aligned with your values, give you a self-esteem boost and get you closer to your goals.

●— PUTTING IT INTO PRACTICE: YOUR HVAS

As an exercise, set a timer for 15 minutes.

Now choose three of your five core values to start. Then come up with three HVAs for each that takes the concept of your value and converts it into an actionable, livable task.

Ideally, these are short actions you can take in five minutes or less at the start of your day. Then go to your calendar and schedule just three of them each day for the next three days. Then make an appointment to repeat this exercise. You can make this a daily practice to identify HVAs each morning *or* come up with enough HVAs for all five of your core values so you can get on a weekly schedule—the choice is yours.

For several examples of how I and some clients use HVAs, go to cbobbook.com/tools.

ONE MORE STEP

Mark LeBlanc also tells a story about his first pilgrimage on El Camino de Santiago in Europe, and it made a huge impression on me.

The Camino is a 500-mile walk visiting holy sites through three countries, culminating at the shrine of the apostle St. James the Great in Galicia, Spain. You carry everything on your back and you camp and stay with other pilgrims and hosts along the way.

Mark says that he had been thinking about this trip for years. And then planning for a few more. And it's only because Mark is who he is that this didn't just stay on his "someday" list but actually happened.

So, in the story, he gets to France, which is the most common place to start the Camino, and he's a couple of miles into his first day when the second-guessing and regrets creep in.

He suddenly feels lonely, his feet hurt, and he's starting to feel a bit silly. Those 200 lies come flooding in.

"What the hell am I doing here?" he asks himself with every step until he gives up and sits down on a low stone wall. "This is the stupidest idea I've ever had. I don't want to walk 500 miles to Spain all by myself! I'm done."

He was at dinner that night with a few other walkers, probably looking as miserable as he felt, when a woman from England, Judith, shared her best pearl of wisdom.

"I have learned one thing," she said, smiling at him. "No matter how miserable you are or how badly your feet are bruised and bleeding – you can always take one more step."

Mark freely shares with audiences around the world that he hung on to her words for over a million steps across northern Spain.

In the end, he walked all 500 miles. And by the time he was finished, he was so inspired that he booked his next trip. He's since returned multiple times and completed the Camino every time. He even wrote a book about his experience, titled *Never Be the Same*.

That experience changed his life, and it all started with just one more step.

For Mark, there was no doubt in his mind as he planned that first trip that he wanted to do it. But when he got there, his feelings changed. The distance between what he imagined it would feel like and what it actually felt like was just enough room for the 200 lies to move in.

I'm guessing you've had a similar experience in your life as well. You've been inspired to do something and you're off to the races. You're eager and enthusiastic and planning up a storm.

Then the other demands on your life show up. All that excitement is replaced by second-guesses and your 200 lies. Your eagerness fades.

You feel yourself getting bogged down. Maybe you feel silly or tired, and you just want to quit.

It's so much more comfortable to stay safe in the security of our everyday lives. We don't have to stretch ourselves. We could stay exactly where we are and never change at all.

This is why, very often, it takes a major shake-up in our lives—a divorce, the death of a loved one, or the loss of a job—to get us out of our routines and into something we've been saying we want to do for years.

We don't like discomfort, but it moves us from where we don't want to be to where we do.

In the Unstuff Your Life System, we've gamified taking one more step and called it #1morething.

Participants are encouraged to look around and see what's one more thing they can do to speed up their decluttering and build better habits. Is it washing the dishes before bedtime so you wake up to a clean sink? Folding the laundry instead of leaving it in the bottom of the basket?

This one hack has changed thousands of lives and has never taken longer than five minutes to do.

So what's one more thing you can do to move yourself a bit closer to one of your goals? How can you take one more step right now and every day?

THE BOTTOM LINE

Mindset matters. Attitude matters. The way you think about your life matters as much as the things you do. Maybe more, because how you think and feel determines what you do.

Approach your busy-ness from a state of abundance, and you'll find that your time is much easier to manage than if you approach it like an all-or-nothing death match.

Learn to recognize the moments when your statements, thoughts, and actions are out of alignment. Those are some of your 200 lies, and they don't serve you. They only keep you stuck.

If you don't carve out time for the activities that are highest value and matter most to you, they won't happen. Think of a jar that's already full of sand—there's no way you'll fit any golf balls in there.

What *are* those golf balls? What's most important to you, and what will move the needle forward on the goals that correspond to each of your core values?

Leverage your tools—your timer, stopwatch, and calendar—to measure, schedule, and plan. Add your HVAs, and your golf balls, to your calendar first, and let the less urgent and important stuff fill in around them. Don't worry, you won't forget—other people won't let you if the little stuff is important to them.

And if it's not important to you or them, it's fine if it doesn't get done.

Get comfortable with at least a bit of discomfort. It's how we grow. What's one more step you can take, today, to get you closer to your goals? What's #1morething?

Not five more things, or trying to squeeze more into an already-busy schedule. Just one more thing you can do before bedtime that builds self-esteem and momentum.

CHAPTER RECAP

Good time management does not require fancy or expensive tools. You can accomplish everything you need and want to do with these three readily available tools:

- Timer
- Stopwatch
- Calendar

THE TIMER

Use this tool to shift from narrative goals to math-based goals. Going forward, instead of declaring that you will work on something until it is finished—say you're going to work on it for X amount of time, ideally from 15 minutes to 3 hours. When the timer goes off, if you have worked without interruption, you have accomplished your goal.

THE STOPWATCH

The timer is used when you don't know how long it takes you to do something, primarily recurring tasks. To capture that data, you will use a stopwatch. Start it when you begin the task and stop it when you finish. Record that timing. Then, the next time you schedule a similar or the same task, you won't over- or underestimate how long to budget for the task.

CALENDAR

The calendar is your roadmap for life, at least as far as time is concerned, and following it is how you will drive each of your days forward. If something isn't in your calendar, it is unlikely to happen. So schedule all recurring and one-off tasks in your calendar. Digital or paper, the format doesn't matter to your success. Just consider that the benefits of a digital calendar are that it's easy to update, free, and available to share with anyone who also needs to know what you are doing on any given day. But if you love a paper calendar, use one. What matters is that you use it consistently to schedule everything and anything that you are committed to doing.

Beyond these three essential tools, there are a few concepts that will help you make the most of your time and the rest of this book.

TO-DO LISTS

To-do lists are not a time management tool—you could consider them a time management container. They're a way to get everything out of your head and onto paper so nothing gets missed or forgotten.

Any item on your to-do list won't get done until you pull it off your list and assign a specific date and time for doing it. This is why the calendar is a foundational tool.

TIME BUCKETS

Time buckets as I use and teach them are just a visual way of categorizing similar kinds of tasks. Some people find it easier to visualize dropping (or grouping) tasks that all have something in common into a container rather than putting them on a list. It gives the tasks a particular kind of weight and dimension that is harder to sense from a line item on a list. It's also a way of using the second leg of the Organizational Triangle, Like with Like, to organize your tasks.

This way, when you start to prioritize, you are only evaluating similar tasks within each category, or time bucket, to determine its relative urgency and importance compared with other items in the same bucket.

If you arrange things visually, time buckets will help you "see" similar tasks as you sort them together.

To prevent time buckets from overflowing, be conscious of what and how much you put in each one.

THE PARETO PRINCIPLE (OR THE 80/20 RULE)

The Pareto Principle was named for a 19th-century Italian economist, Vilfredo Pareto, who discovered that 80 percent of the land in Italy was owned by 20 percent of the population. What he found even more curious was that this 80/20 split appeared in lots of other places. For example, 80 percent of a company's income can often be attributed to 20 percent of its best clients or customers.

In the context of your life, you can use the Pareto Principle to help you prioritize and get the big things, the golf balls mentioned in the previous chapter, done.

HIGH-VALUE ACTIVITIES

Think of HVAs (high-value activities) as mini golf balls or chunked-up bits of a golf ball—important and also short and quick to do. They could be work tasks like calling a prospect or sending an email, or personal activities like doing 10 burpees before breakfast or meditating for five minutes when you wake up.

We'll come back to these tools and concepts throughout the book, so get familiar with them now. You'll find additional resources at cbob-book.com/tools.

Gather your timer, stopwatch, and calendar; name your time buckets; and then start to sketch out personal and professional HVAs.

When you feel busy, it's easy to push the most important tasks to the back burner because you don't have the energy or concentration you need in the moment to give them the attention they require. And then you undermine your success further by telling yourself one of your 200 lies—that you will definitely do these things "when you have more time."

The problem with this "strategy" is that (1) it's not a strategy, (2) it delays the most important activities while you busy yourself with things that, in 30 minutes, 30 days, or 30 months, won't even have mattered, and (3) you will never have this elusive "more time" if you don't actively prioritize setting it aside now.

As discussed in the previous chapter as well, let's reverse that behavior and use an actual strategy instead. Rather than overloading your schedule with inconsequential yet somehow needling little tasks, start your day by setting aside enough time to attack your prioritized highest-value activities first. That way you'll either get them done or at least take a big bite out of them before the day gets away from you.

Chapter 3

The 8 Deadly Time Thieves

"The robb'd that smiles steals something from the thief . . ."
William Shakespeare, *Othello*

"There is only one sin, and that is theft."
Khaled Hosseini

There are almost as many different ways to lose time as there are people.

But, because we're all human, those ways tend to follow patterns and fall into similar categories.

Let's group the biggest and most frequent offenders of our modern age into the 8 Deadly Time Thieves.

The Roman Catholic Church maintains that the seven deadly sins are vices that spur other sins and create a pattern of immoral behavior. I'm not about to heap any guilt on you, but in this case, it's a useful precedent.

The 8 Deadly Time Thieves have a lot in common with the seven deadlies. They aren't the only ways to waste time—but they *are* insidious and they often lead to other time wasters.

And because almost all of them are tied to common activities, it can be hard to distinguish when we've stopped being efficient and slid into soul-sucking time wasting. That usually happens after a bit of time has passed and we realize that we've been down a rather long and narrow rabbit hole.

Shortening the distance between conscious tasking and a sleepwalking version of the same thing is one of the goals of this book.

I don't expect that you will never waste time again—that seems unrealistic.

What I want for you, for me, and for us all, is that we become so attuned and alert to our behavior that when any of the 8 Deadlies starts to take hold, we can quickly recognize it and stop it.

Then we can mindfully return or pivot to a task or activity that actually serves us, rather than burning through our time unconsciously.

Paying attention and being mindful are required if we're going to take charge of our lives and direct them with any intention.

Remember: you are responsible for everything that you do in your life—you're not necessarily to blame for your circumstances. Regardless of how or why something has happened, you are responsible for what you do next.

It's like that quote from Charles Swindoll: "Life is 10 percent what happens to me and 90 percent how I react to it."

HOW EASY IT IS TO LIE TO OURSELVES

Let's say you're running to an appointment.

You stop to answer one more email before you race out the door, and now you're feeling a bit anxious and agitated.

You've done the math and if everything goes perfectly between your front door and your destination, you'll make it right on time or maybe two to three minutes late . . . which you tell yourself—one of your 200 lies—is an acceptable window of error.

From the outside, sure—few people will fault you for showing up a few minutes late.

But, really, what are you doing?

You knew you were cutting it close when you decided to answer that email instead of leaving with enough time to not feel anxious.

The fact that you can come up with what you consider to be an unassailable explanation doesn't make it any less of a lie.

But what happens if there's an accident up ahead or they're doing roadwork?

Any unexpected delay will make you later than you hoped and later than your "legit" excuse can cover.

At this point, do you scheme harder to come up with a better excuse? Or tell the truth about choosing to do something else instead of leaving on time and accept the consequences?

When you're calling to apologize and alert them to your delay, do you also make a mental note about what just happened so it doesn't happen again?

Or walk yourself back and minimize the impact, writing it off as an isolated incident?

Do you cling to the story that of course you respect other people's time as much as your own, even though, based on your behavior, others might not agree?

Whatever you learn from this series of events, the point is not to torment yourself—that's not likely to prompt better choices. Shame is, to use Brené Brown's words, "more likely to be the source of destructive, hurtful behavior than the solution or cure."[17]

The point is to own whatever self-centeredness directed your choices and amend your behavior so you make a different choice going forward.

If you can tell the truth to yourself about what just happened, you can also forgive yourself for being human and self-involved and then pivot into using the time that's left as productively as possible.

When you're honest with yourself, you can get beyond that feeling of being stuck. You don't need to call yourself an asshole any more than you need to pretend you didn't just steal some time from someone for your own benefit.

You'll also stop yourself from investing more time in cooking up a "good" excuse and instead let it go and move on.

When you aren't honest with yourself, the feelings start to get sticky and it becomes harder to let go.

You may flip-flop between feeling bad about your choice and shaming yourself, and justifying why it doesn't represent a pattern of behavior or why this time was different. Back and forth you go, burning through time and indulging in a bit of drama and exaggerated feelings.

Shaming yourself for poor judgment is like paying for something twice.

Instead of beating up on yourself and feeling upset, what if you chose to use the time in the car to meditate? Or listen to some calming music or an audiobook, or return a phone call?

One thing's for sure: you will be in the car until you are not in the car.

So do you want to spend that time consciously or get lost in a sea of emotion and "check out" as a coping mechanism for feelings that you instigated through your initial behavior?

The irony is that after the feelings first surface, choosing to dig in and relive them probably makes you more miserable than you may have felt just observing them in the first place. This is a cousin to complaining about something more than once, which we discussed in Chapter 2.

A Buddhist principle is that pain is a part of life; suffering is optional. Keep that in mind when things go awry so you don't pick at a wound looking for some stimulation.

Traffic is outside your control—leaving the house on time or shaming yourself until you feel like you've suffered enough to adequately pay for your choice are both on you.

Likewise, bosses, coworkers, kids, spouses, strangers on the street, governments, weather . . . all of these will behave as they will, often beyond your sphere of influence.

Which is fine because you've got enough to do just managing yourself.

Even if you trade your time for money for eight or more hours a day, no one has absolute control over you and your actions—you do.

But the story you tell yourself may go something like this: *I need this job. I have to put up with this crap even though it makes me crazy (or upset, angry, sad, etc.). I'm trapped here by circumstance. I wish I could get away from this but I can't.*

I'm not implying it will be easy to interrupt that story.

Or that if you're working for minimum wage or less that it won't require a tremendous amount of effort and energy to continue working in a culture that causes you pain *and* search for your next opportunity. You may have to exert yourself to the limit of what you think you can tolerate.

Making the best decision involves weighing the costs of staying against the costs of leaving as objectively and thoroughly as possible.

One situation sounds like the slow and steady death of your spirit, the other like stretching yourself for a limited amount of time with the promise of eventual relief—which will be easier to recover from?

Whatever you choose to do, you've got to keep the focus on yourself if your efforts to tame the 8 Deadly Time Thieves are going to pay off.

COMMON CAUSES OF LOST TIME

Here's a starter set of the most common ways we lose time in our modern lives. The 8 Deadlies are included in this list:

- Complaining rather than advocating
- Commuting
- Gossiping

- Being interrupted by others
- Doing other people's work, thinking you're a team player
- Doing other people's work, thinking it's easier or faster than teaching them how to do it themselves
- Watching TV, thinking you're doing research
- Hanging out with negative people
- Getting lost down a rabbit hole doing research, thinking you're being thorough
- Not putting things away in the moment and creating clutter (piling instead of filing)
- Picking fights and antagonizing others, often disguised as constructive criticism
- Multitasking
- Playing video games obsessively
- Eating your feelings, especially when you're not hungry
- Making empty promises to yourself and others
- Waiting for magic or inspiration to motivate you
- Solving the same problem more than twice without documenting how you did it
- Overcommitting
- Making random stacks of papers without corralling them or prioritizing them
- Criticizing yourself beyond noting a weakness or an area for improvement
- Adopting an overly dramatic approach to life
- Underestimating the time needed to complete a project
- Overestimating the time needed to complete a project
- Planning poorly
- Aggressively demanding perfection at any cost
- Procrastinating
- Attending unnecessary or poorly run meetings
- Sending or answering email randomly
- Getting lost on social media platforms

As you read this list, it's important to acknowledge but not dwell on any activities you engage in, regardless of how often you do them.

It's equally important that you own the stories you tell yourself for either why you do them or why they aren't a waste of time. This step, as much as the loss of time itself, is crucial.

Self-examination requires us to look honestly, accurately, and compassionately at our thoughts, feelings, and actions. You're not on trial, so you don't have to defend anything. But if you can't see it, you can't fix it.

Reclaiming your time is also not a contest, so resist the urge to read the list and exclaim, "Ha! I don't do *that*," as if you're superior to someone who does.

I don't play video games at all—that doesn't make me better than someone who does.

I'm certainly guilty of telling myself that it's easier to just do a task than taking the time to teach someone how to do it, even though I know that investing that time once would pay dividends forever when I successfully delegate the task away.

Sometimes in the moment it seems faster and easier to just do it yourself. In hindsight that is almost always penny-wise, pound-foolish.

So spotting your 200 lies and getting honest about what you're actually doing rather than what you might tell yourself you're doing is one of the fastest ways to set yourself free.

THE 8 DEADLY TIME THIEVES

Any of the behaviors above can steal your time—the 8 Deadlies are just the worst:

- Interruptions
- Multitasking
- Overcommitting
- Poor Planning
- Email
- Meetings
- Social Media
- Procrastination

They don't always appear in this order, they don't all arrive together or leave at the same time, and they certainly don't show up the same way for each of us.

But these eight are killers.

You might be interrupted one way today and another way tomorrow. What worked last week to shut down a time thief might not work next month.

You'll find specific techniques to deal with each thief in the upcoming chapters, but don't get too attached to any of them. Just like updates for software, over time the thieves and what works to shut them down will change.

So rather than searching for a magic bullet or one-time fix, the best and most consistent solution is much simpler and universal: staying alert and not lying to yourself.

I put the Big P—Procrastination—at the end of the list because it's often talked about as the ultimate cause of lost time. As if the solution to procrastination were its own holy grail.

What you'll find in Chapter 11 is how surprisingly mundane and fixable procrastination is.

So don't build it up into a giant scary monster in your mind. Like the abominable snowman in the old stop-motion *Rudolph the Red Nose Reindeer* Christmas special, it's mostly bark, not bite. And once you pull its teeth out, it's harmless.

SAVE THE DRAMA FOR THE STAGE

If you are at all prone to being dramatic in your self-assessments, you'll quickly learn to knock it off and settle down. Living at that pitch is exhausting. You can't sustain such a high degree of upset or agitation and not pay for it with your time, energy, and focus.

And no one really cares about how any of the 8 Deadlies are kicking your butt unless it directly impacts them. They may say they care, but that's probably one of *their* 200 lies.

Also, hysterics are not what make you charming or fun to be around—they just get in the way of solving the real problem.

They say whatever is hysterical is historical, so you'll get much further faster figuring out what's really going on when you react that strongly.

Getting cut off in traffic or enduring a particularly long wait online for tech support is frustrating for sure. But neither of them is cancer or global warming.

So see if you can figure out the first time you felt disrespected or invisible—that's probably what's triggering such a strong response. The asshole who got into your lane without signaling is just the most recent occurrence of that. He doesn't deserve that much of your time or energy.

Pay particular attention anytime you refer to things in all-or-nothing terms or use the words "always" or "never." That's likely to be one of your 200 lies, because few things are that black or white.

This won't always be easy because you're undoing unconscious habits that may have been around for years. But it is simple.

Each chapter will focus on one of the thieves and dissect what they look like, how to spot them, and—most important—how to stop them.

For now, here's a quick overview of the villains we're working against, each of which is covered in its own chapter.

INTERRUPTIONS

Interruptions take many forms, and they're often wrapped in a story about connecting with others or being approachable and available. That might look like a colleague stopping by to ask a quick question or even just to gossip. Your phone pinging you, either with an alarm you set or a random notification, your dog asking to go out, your child asking for a snack—all interruptions.

Any unplanned intrusion into what you had already scheduled qualifies, even if it's "urgent," particularly when it's someone else's urgency and not yours.

Note that interruptions are external and different from distractions, which are self-created.

MULTITASKING

You might think you're listening to the conference call while organizing your sock drawer, but you aren't.

You're monitoring both activities, not really present for either. Your skill with multitasking is not your superpower, but it is one of your 200 lies, because our brains aren't wired for it.

We'll explore why and how the brain evolved, and look at how doing just one thing at a time is actually faster and more effective.

OVERCOMMITTING

This is what happens when you say yes to too many things in too small a window.

Victims of this thief often start resenting doing even the things they like to do, because they feel overwhelmed and out of control everywhere in their lives.

Simple math tells us when we put too many things on our calendar, we either have to let some things go or drive ourselves to exhaustion to complete everything.

POOR PLANNING

This time thief comes in multiple forms. Not thinking tasks and projects all the way through and just winging it; under- or overestimating how long things take based on feelings rather than data; not using your calendar to budget time and attention—these are all examples of poor planning.

You also can't manage what you don't measure, so you'll learn more about time triage and the Pareto Principle, time buckets, and to-do lists.

Chapter 7, on poor planning, is perhaps the most important chapter in the book.

To quote Ben Franklin, "If you fail to plan, you plan to fail."

EMAIL

You know that sinking feeling you get when you check your email first thing in the morning and it's all bad news? That's what it feels like when a time thief sucks away your energy and momentum. Kind of like the dementors in Harry Potter.

Email is often a seriously inefficient form of communication.

Just think of how many back-and-forth exchanges it takes to answer a simple question and its follow-up questions. Then imagine one five-minute phone call where you could have covered everything from start to finish once.

Then multiply that by 100, the average number of emails we each get every day. That's the scale of how aggressively email gobbles up time.

MEETINGS

Not all meetings are time thieves, but bad meetings always are.

Meetings can and should be productive opportunities to engage, collaborate, and achieve common goals.

But when they're unnecessary, unstructured, or unfocused, they are one of the most expensive time wasters in the corporate world, to the tune of $399 billion a year in the US alone.[18]

SOCIAL MEDIA

Kind of like email, but worse.

Imagine a town square with everyone yelling at the same time, clamoring for your attention. Then picture yourself standing there, too, yelling just as loud or running around high-fiving, hugging, or frowning at everyone else in the square.

With social media, the time wasting happens almost as soon as you start scrolling, even if you tell yourself you're catching up with friends, colleagues, or the competition.

It's hard to imagine anything else you would invite into your life that could more quickly and negatively impact your mood and well-being.

PROCRASTINATION

Procrastination gets a bad rap for good reason—but it's really not that complicated or scary. It happens whenever, either consciously or unconsciously, you avoid a task you *should* be doing or indulge in a task you should have stopped 15 minutes ago but didn't because you told yourself a story about taking care of yourself and feeling good . . . and because, damn it, you deserve it.

Of course, it's all your time, so you can do whatever you want with it. But the irony is that indulging in something you should have stopped 15 minutes ago has the same negative impact on your overall time management as if you blew off a task you didn't want to do. Ouch.

BIOLOGY, HUMAN NATURE, AND CHANGE

Changing behaviors and building new habits isn't complicated, but it can be uncomfortable. It also means paying enough attention that you don't operate on autopilot and do what you usually do. Because when you do what you usually do, you'll get what you usually get.

How far are you willing to go to make a change? How uncomfortable are you willing to be in the short term for permanent long-term gain?

It may be helpful to remember that we're wired to avoid pain at all costs. And we'll be fighting our inherent laziness, too, biologically speaking. We have survived this long because we are experts at conserving energy.

So we're designed to run from pain and do as little as possible.

You may be thinking, "Well, damned if I do and damned if I don't," but try looking at it this way.

Which pain is less tolerable: the pain of doing nothing and living with your current conditions or the pain of building some muscles and a few good or better habits?

I don't like working out. I love to sit and think. I love teaching and talking. I'm very comfortable from the neck up.

I was also a professional drummer for many years and a trained actor and dancer. So it's not like I'm disconnected from my body or uncomfortable being in it and using it.

But picking up and putting down dumbbells holds almost no fascination for me. I'd only run if someone were chasing me.

So what to do?

I want to be fit and take care of my body so it lasts as long as it can with as few problems as possible. I'm also vain enough that I want to look good with and without clothes on.

But I don't want to do the thing that will give me those results.

So I work out with a trainer three times a week. Not because I want to work out, but because I want the result of having worked out.

Because the pain of spending a few bucks and not showing up is worse than the pain of doing 60-second planks and swinging a kettlebell.

And I always feel better afterward.

But you should know that every time, and I mean every time, I'm about to get on Zoom, the first thought that comes to me is not "This is awesome, I can't wait to see Michael and work out," but "This sucks. I've got a ton of work to do. How can I get out of this today?"

I'm just being honest.

I remind myself that winners do what they have to do. And I want to be a winner today. So I do the thing I don't want to do to get the thing I want to have.

Les Brown says it this way: "To be successful, you must be willing to do the things today others won't do in order to have the things tomorrow others won't have."

Stated either way, I know it's easier for me to do what has to be done when someone else is holding me accountable.

Left to my own devices, I will tell any number of lies to get out of doing something I don't want to do.

But one of my core values is integrity, so I remind myself that I made a commitment to Michael and myself and I don't want to be out of integrity.

I'm not going to promise you that you're ever going to love doing what you need to do to set yourself free. But I will promise you that you'll love the freedom you get from doing it.

I also don't want to scare you or turn you off from doing the work. You may come to love it. I used to hate doing laundry and I love it now. I used to be intimidated by tools and I love fixing things now.

James Clear in *Atomic Habits* talks about changing your image of yourself as a way of changing your habits.[19]

So maybe I can change my image of myself from being a nerd and an egghead to being a jock who loves to work out. I just haven't gotten there yet.

COMFORT IS RELATIVE AND OFTEN OVERRATED

You're going to concentrate on something every day, right?

And if food, clothing, and shelter are taken care of, how much more comfort do you need?

Why not focus on something that will deliver a larger payoff than constantly monitoring your comfort level, like ending the habit of letting yourself off the hook.

Because another fork in the road is deciding what you are going to pursue: comfort at any cost or your dreams.

I'm not saying that pursuing your dreams requires you to be miserable or to suffer, but if you won't even consider any discomfort, you're probably going to stay right where you are.

I also realize that the comfort we're discussing here does not include the kind of comfort some people may be pursuing to just feel safe on the planet—and I hope you can tell the difference as well.

So, assuming you are the first kind of comfortable already, the quickest way forward is addressing your mindset.

That's how you will counteract your biological imperative to avoid risk and exertion unless it's absolutely necessary.

Imagine a mental place where you are not rushing or stressed or anxious. Where you are engaged in tasks and responsibilities—but not more of them than serve you. A place where you are aligned with what's important to you, what you need to do each day, and when you'll do it.

A place where you easily and confidently take charge of your own life.

Compare that mindset with your current state and then let's take the steps needed to close any gap between them.

GOING BEYOND TRADITIONAL METHODS

Most traditional time management systems will only get you so far. Maybe you've tried some of them, like the Pomodoro (tomato timer) Technique or Getting Things Done (GTD).

Often, these work in the beginning when change seems easy and exciting, and then fail when life happens, meaning something unexpected occurs or you don't see results quick enough.

At that point, most of us fall back into old habits—if we're not going to get the results we want and expect, we may as well choose comfort and familiarity, right? It's easier that way.

Maybe you thought you weren't "trying hard enough" or you were "doing it wrong" when you couldn't sustain a new system.

The real reason most of these systems don't work is that they require additional time to keep them running. Remember our plate-spinning friend from Ed Sullivan?

For example, the GTD method involves extra steps to maintain it, in addition to the tasks it promises to make easier—who has time to maintain a "tickler" file?

But the two-minute rule? That is golden. So use what works and toss the rest.

HOW TO THINK LIKE A TIME HACKER

- Study your current behavior and habits. Observe without judging yourself negatively for any place you're falling short, but do analyze where failures occur and what's causing them.
- Track your energy levels—when are they high and when are they low?
- Is there any pattern to when you feel in control of your time or when you feel helpless?
- Don't get attached to your expectations around results. Consistency pays off every time, but if you're constantly evaluating your progress, you're almost guaranteed to undervalue how far you've come compared with where you think you should be.
- Let nothing be so sacred that you aren't willing to let it go or change it when a better way becomes clear.

THE ORGANIZATIONAL TRIANGLE

If you've read my first book, *Unstuff Your Life!*, you already know this tool. And if you haven't, you can learn more about it and my other books at my website, andrewmellen.com/books.

The Organizational Triangle is helpful for physical objects and it's also useful in reframing your approach to time and the 8 Deadlies.

Like any triangle, the Organizational Triangle has three sides:

- One Home for Everything
- Like with Like
- Something In, Something Out

And this is how you use it with time.

ONE HOME FOR EVERYTHING

That would be your calendar. Everything you do starts with an appointment on your calendar.

You want to write a book or learn to play the piano? Make appointments with yourself and then keep them. Saying "I'm going to write each day" without scheduling time to pick up your pen or use your keyboard means you're relying on your memory or inspiration to get you writing—both of which can fail to show up when you need them.

LIKE WITH LIKE

This is useful for batching tasks. You burn through a tremendous amount of energy by shifting tasks rapidly. Your brain doesn't like to work that hard. So bouncing around between projects involving different skill sets will tire you out fast.

You might like novelty, but that's not the best way to achieve it.

It's much better to batch like tasks together as much as possible.

When I was writing this book, I only got on the internet to research a point I was making or find a link to share that supports my claim. Otherwise, all browser windows were closed and I saved checking email and other admin tasks for when I finished for the day.

SOMETHING IN, SOMETHING OUT

We all need a healthy balance of rest, play, physical activity, and brain work in our day. Not every day will be identical in how time is allotted to these categories. But once you've reached a state of "time equilibrium," meaning the day is fully booked, you don't want to add additional appointments—you just want to shift around the allotments.

So you can say yes to something new as long as you're willing to redistribute time among your existing tasks, reschedule something for another day, delegate something to someone else, or completely remove something from your calendar.

Too often we just pack more into the day without releasing anything at the same time—and that creates "busy," the time equivalent of clutter.

THE BOTTOM LINE

There are lots of ways we lose time. Some are more common—and troublesome—than others.

A positive and expansive mindset is your best tool as you approach any time thief, deadly or otherwise.

Shame is a lousy motivator—find something else to propel you forward.

You're probably more comfortable than you know or acknowledge. Get clear on that now so you can spend less time pursuing comfort and more time pursuing your other goals.

Consider two other books as additional sources as you're trying to build new habits: *The Four Agreements* by don Miguel Ruiz and *Atomic Habits* by James Clear.

When the unexpected happens, remember the second of The Four Agreements: Don't Take Anything Personally.

For the most part, things just happen near you and sometimes splash onto you. Focus less on the problem and more on the solution. Now that something has happened, what do you want to do about it? That is what you have control over.

CHAPTER RECAP

There are many ways in which we lose or waste time, but eight of them are particularly harmful, and I call them the 8 Deadly Time Thieves. They are:

- Interruptions
- Multitasking
- Overcommitting
- Poor Planning
- Email
- Meetings
- Social Media
- Procrastination

Eliminating any or all of these time thieves from your life will involve some work and may involve some discomfort. But that's okay, because the upside is less friction and a clearer path toward your dreams. Seems like a fair trade, right?

Traditional time management systems tend to work in the beginning and then fail when life "gets in the way," which usually means that something unexpected happens or your impatience is increasing because you aren't seeing results to match your needs or expectations.

You probably weren't "doing it wrong." These systems tend to fail because they require additional time and extra steps to keep them running—and who's got time for that? So rather than following any system to the letter, use what works for you and toss the rest.

To think like a time hacker, study your current habits without judgment, analyzing where friction and failures happen and their root causes. Don't get attached to either the failures or the expectations; just observe what, when, and how you do what you do, and the results you get from those efforts. Change whatever isn't working, keep what is, and look for ways to streamline your successes to gain even more traction and get more time back.

The Organizational Triangle is a tool I use with clients to clear clutter. You can watch a short video to learn more about it on my YouTube channel. It is also helpful when reframing your approach to time and attacking the 8 Deadlies.

The three sides of the Organizational Triangle for time are:

- One Home for Everything: Every task you're actively working on lives in your calendar; all tasks not yet assigned live in your time buckets.
- Like with Like: All tasks live in their common time buckets; common tasks are batched together to save time and reduce context switching when executing them.
- Something In, Something Out: If you say yes to something new, you have to find time for it. That may mean saying no to something already on your calendar so you don't overextend yourself and fall back into "busy."

Chapter 4

Interruptions

*"People who say it cannot be done should not interrupt
those of us who are doing it."*
Unknown

Until you tame interruptions, your ability to stay focused is always
vulnerable and easily compromised.

And what makes interruptions so hard to stop is that they involve
other people and require you to establish consistent and workable,
meaning doable, boundaries.

If you're thinking, "What's the big deal? So what if someone interrupts
me? I can quickly get back to what I was doing," you're mistaken.

Time magazine reported that, on a typical day, workers are interrupted about 7 times an hour or 56 times a day—and 80 percent of those
interruptions are considered trivial. A study by Basex Research done
in 2005 quantified the cost of interruptions to the US economy to be
$588 billion a year.[20]

As you'll see below, even in WFH (work from home) situations, interruptions are rampant.

Not to mention that an interruption is literally someone stealing your
time. And we often let that happen without any resistance.

You invite interruptions tacitly by keeping your door open. You do it actively by enabling notifications on your devices, including the ringer on your phone.

And you make it worse when you drop everything to respond to any request immediately—regardless of what you might have been doing at the time.

You can tell yourself one of your 200 lies—that you don't want to appear unapproachable or cold.

You can point to the culture at work, claiming it's all about "open doors" and being accessible.

But, really, $588 billion in the US alone. Interruptions suck.

If the choice were between your happiness and productivity or accessibility, which would you choose? Because that is what's at stake.[21]

Look, there are times when you'll need to be interrupted—there is an actual emergency or crisis, or the dog seriously has to pee—but most interruptions can be anticipated *or* your participation can wait.

A mom at one of our workshops told the group that when she's working from home she tells her kids, "When mommy is working, unless you are bleeding out, you can wait until she is off the call to get her attention."

You might think she's a coldhearted witch—I think she's got great boundaries. And teaching her kids how and when to ask for help will teach them patience and how to maintain focus, and serve them well as they mature and want to get things done in their own lives.

Growing up with electronic devices in their hands, our next few generations are having their attention fractured before they even know it.[22] Sitting still and concentrating is becoming more and more difficult.

BOUNDARIES ARE YOUR FRIEND

Without healthy and stable boundaries, you have zero control over your day.

So when you stop interruptions, you're building a firewall between you, your calendar, and everything else.

It's the simplest and most direct way to stay focused on the goals, tasks, and activities that matter most to you.

Consider this. As discussed in Chapter 2, we're interrupted by communications technology every 10 minutes. And for every interruption, it takes an average of 23 minutes to recover. That means that 2 interruptions + 2 recoveries = up to 1 full hour of time lost.

But remember, you're likely to be interrupted another three times during each hour, so the impact is even greater.

When you add up all the interruptions and attempted recoveries, you can see why, at quitting time, you may be thinking, "I've been crazy busy all day and I've gotten nothing done."

And this is how insidious some of your 200 lies can be when it comes to interruptions.

The phone rings and you tell yourself, "It'll only take me five minutes to answer the call and then they'll leave me alone."

Or a notification pops up on your screen and you say, "I'll just check to see if it's urgent. Worst case, I'll answer one email and then get right back to what I was doing."

But the net time cost is so much higher when you factor in the following:

- The lost time on what you were doing before you task-switched
- The time needed to regain your focus and resume your previous task
- The pattern of acceptable interruptions that this sets up or reinforces

Protecting your time isn't the same as being ungenerous with it—which takes us back to open doors, accessibility, and perception.

Office hours for university professors makes them appear accessible and allows anyone to get their attention during those times, so why does the same protocol at the office seem restrictive or impersonal?

The more control you have over how you spend your time, the more you're able to direct it toward the people and activities that you value—whether that's the team at work or your family at home.

As you exert your boundaries, the internal story (one of your 200 lies) will say that you're selfish and self-centered—and that may be echoed in subtle and not-so-subtle ways by the people bumping into those boundaries.

Those people are likely to have some feelings in response to being told "no" or "not now" and then make their upset about you.

This is compounded at work, where the culture typically evolves like a patchwork quilt. It's stitched together over time with ideas and concepts introduced to improve teamwork and leadership—but randomly, without a clear design.

Individually, any of these ideas may produce results. Open doors can create greater accessibility; open floor plans can foster collaboration; Scrum, Six Sigma, and Kaizen can increase productivity.

But just because they look good on paper or in an online seminar doesn't mean they will solve your specific challenges or be a good fit with the existing culture.

Open-door policies and open floor plans are sometimes chosen more for their optics than what they actually deliver.

Leaders sometimes insist on implementing the latest fad despite resistance or even documented proof of its ineffectiveness simply because it looks good to corporate management or can be exploited by the marketing team.

When mashed together or layered on top of each other, some of these concepts clash and even neutralize any gains. And create brand-new problems when deployed.

The data proves that while collaboration can go up in open floor plans, concentration and productivity consistently drop by over 30 percent[23]— how much more important than productivity is collaboration to the success of *your* business?

Often when I'm brought into a company to solve a productivity issue, the problem can be traced back to a failure of communication, culture, or system. The solution isn't adding something new—it's removing something broken or clarifying something easily overlooked because it was so obvious.

MINDSET AND MORTALITY

And whether individually or company-wide, we often resist saying no simply because we don't like the way it feels.

That is a glass-half-empty mindset.

It is focused on what you're saying no to and all the reactions to that "no."

A glass-half-full mindset is focused on what you're gaining *by* saying no—primarily more time for something you value more.

Which leads us back to the mom and her kids mentioned above. At first, the kids might have a strong reaction to being denied instant access to their mom whenever they want. What a mean mom!

But she knows that at that moment, her kids are not in any danger. And that by focusing on her work, she's keeping a roof over their heads and food in their bellies. Not to mention teaching her kids an important lesson about delayed gratification. Maybe she's a smart mom?

Saying "no" or "not now" is one of the simplest ways to say yes to something you've already committed to and determined was important.

It's not easy or fun being an adult sometimes and accepting that while you *can* do anything you want, you can't do it all at the same time.

And that also means you can't do everything unless you've also figured out how to live forever.

So, while accepting the limitations of being human means accepting your mortality as the very foundation of every other choice, being human with a kick-ass mindset means you get to do some incredible things while you're here.

FOMO (fear of missing out) is a pervasive, collective mindfuck that is driven by our egos and nurtured by commercial interests that have learned exactly how to exploit our egos' constant hunger for power and prestige.

Of course, interruptions are easier to manage when you work or live by yourself.

So while being single often negatively impacts our lifespan,[24] the good news is we'll be less interrupted until we die.

Wherever you have interdependent relationships or spend time in close proximity to others, your boundaries will be tested.

But there are very few situations where you can't reduce, if not prevent, interruptions. It just takes more effort.

The best and most transparent way to do that is to gently, firmly, and consistently teach people how to approach you and when.

And if this is the first time you're setting up boundaries or updating existing boundaries, tell the truth about why you're doing it—you've got nothing to hide or be ashamed of.

You can also directly address any expectations others may have based on your previous availability.

It may be a little awkward or uncomfortable to plainly state when and how you can be interrupted. But it is definitely not impossible.

Now back to mindset—I'll bet you've already done much harder things in your life so far. Accept that if you're going to get control over your time, you're going to have to create and hold a few boundaries. It doesn't need to be any more fraught than that.

INTERRUPTIONS VS. DISTRACTIONS

As you consider all the ways and times you're interrupted (and your historical role in that), you may be confusing your own distractions with interruptions, so let's clarify the difference.

Interruptions are external—they happen outside of us. Distractions are internal—they are self-generated.

Interruptions look like this:

- A ringing phone
- A colleague stopping by your desk
- Your kid tugging on your sleeve

Distractions look like this:

- Obsessively checking your phone because it hasn't been ringing
- Opening your email in the middle of writing a report because you're "bored" or want to "switch things up"
- Playing one more round of solitaire or swiping through a dating app before putting your phone down to start working

Full transparency—I have done all of the above.

The good news is you can stop distractions immediately by changing your behavior. I removed the solitaire and all dating apps from my phone.

Unless you have a customer service job or other role where being immediately responsive is required, you can silence all your notifications now. In fact, silence anything that can beep or chirp at you so you can concentrate with fewer interruptions.

Then, when you're ready to start work again, use your timer as we discussed in Chapter 2 and start your first uninterrupted block of time.

The Pomodoro Technique is based on working in 25-minute increments with 5 minutes off—which works great for some folks.

But other people might not have 25 uninterrupted minutes to dedicate to a task, or they can't stay focused for 25 minutes because of ADHD or some other condition.

Ultimately, the amount of time you choose is less important than setting a timer to begin with. So, whether you focus for 5, 25, or 45 minutes, the timer is crucial for working on one task or category of tasks at a time.

When the timer goes off, acknowledge it. You just accomplished what you set out to do—work for a specified block of time without interruption.

Are you ready for more or do you want to stretch and take a quick break?

Some say sitting is the new smoking, so don't underestimate moving your body throughout the day.

While writing this book, I consistently set the timer for one or two hours. When it went off, I got up and walked around the room, did 20 pushups, drank some water, or did all of the above and then set the timer for another block of time and climbed back in.

Breaking up your flow can do a few things:

- Prove that you actually can and did work uninterrupted
- Support or reinforce additional improvements you want to make, such as drinking enough water, getting some exercise, or taking a few deep breaths

- Create momentum as you build self-esteem while getting important things done

However you choose to use the break, when you're ready, set your timer and start again.

The important thing is to build the habit of using the timer and working in blocks of time when interruptions are not allowed.

It should become part of your process to put your phone on Do Not Disturb or, even better, leave it in another room entirely. If you're working on a tablet or computer, silence all notifications and close any browser tabs unrelated to the task at hand.

In the beginning, you'll be amazed at what you can get done when you focus your attention on something without interruption. After a while, you'll come to expect these kinds of results.

HOW TO MINIMIZE OR ELIMINATE INTERRUPTIONS

There is only one way to eliminate interruptions. You've got to change any culture that allows them in the first place.

If you've got a story that says you're just a cog in a wheel and have no authority to alter the culture at work, push on that story a bit to see how accurate it is. And if you really can only change yourself, start there. Stop interrupting others and gently push back when someone interrupts you.

Try to enlist any colleagues and management in making the changes needed so everyone can benefit from working without interruptions.

Give them this chapter and then visit cbobbook.com/interruptions and share the latest statistics there on how much productivity improves when interruptions are removed from a culture.

And while you're working to shift the culture at work, start at home immediately. These steps will get you started.

SHIFT THE CULTURE

This means teaching or "training" others how to be self-reliant and respectful of boundaries. It won't happen overnight and you may experience pushback.

People do not like having something—even something unproductive—taken away from them. So you will want to frame this as a win for them, not a loss. Point out that they are gaining skills and confidence in their own ability to solve problems. Downplay any reduction in your availability. And remind them that you are *still* accessible, just not randomly unless there is an emergency. And then spell out what constitutes an emergency so there can be no confusion going forward.

You'll also want to set up how you'll communicate your unavailability. That could be as simple as closing your door, wearing headphones, or hanging a Do Not Disturb sign on your doorknob.

Don't be afraid to make your signals lighthearted—they just have to be used consistently and unambiguously. Make sure everyone understands that while the signal may be playful, you won't be if they break the rules.

Watch out for anyone wired for negative attention or boundary-bashing. You may have to do extra training with them.

You'll also get to observe who adapts well and who needs extra support. If after a decent amount of time, they can't get with the program, they may need to get off the bus or at least into a different seat on the bus.

This may be a major step forward in your company's productivity, so remain curious as you observe who is committed to their own success as well as the business's. You'll also quickly learn who is more interested in being the life of the party when there is no party on the schedule.

ESTABLISH TIME CONSTRAINTS WHEN INTERRUPTED

Shit happens. And when instituting this kind of a cultural overhaul, some interruptions that don't involve a literal fire will still slip through as people build new skills.

When that happens, offer a course correction. Here's one example: "I will make an exception for you now but should this happen again, you will be gently but firmly turned away. We're going to do two things right now: (1) Make a separate appointment so you and I can look at your decision-making process. I want to understand how you may have confused urgency for importance and how we can do better next time. (2) I'm going to set a timer for 15 minutes for this conversation. If at the end of those 15 minutes, you haven't gotten everything you need from me, we'll make another appointment to tie up any loose ends. Is all that clear?"

Then set the timer. If you don't do this, they will stay until *they* are finished. You are training them to be concise and get to the point and to value your time as much as you do.

Remember, too, that your floor is everyone else's ceiling. That means that wherever you let yourself off the hook is where most people will aim for. They will consciously or unconsciously adjust their behavior to meet you where you naturally settle. Few people are driven to exceed that limit, especially if there's no stated or explicit reward for doing so.

They say, "Children listen," and they do. So does your team. They are always observing and evaluating how you do things. Never forget that each of your actions sends a clear signal of what is acceptable and what is not.

It's essential that people understand that any nonurgent task must wait until you're available. And while you're unavailable, they should step up to the best of their ability. The truth is that most things can wait and that many people can figure out the right thing to do when they have to.

LEVERAGE LIKE WITH LIKE FOR TASKS

Use the second leg of the Organizational Triangle to group similar activities together. Whether you're shopping online, running errands, returning phone calls, or working in the yard, one-off tasks are more quickly done when batched with similar tasks.

It's also easier to maintain your focus and a clear boundary when you say, "I'm doing X for the next two hours." Defining a category of activity *and* a quantified block of time creates a far more effective barrier than just saying, "I'm busy right now."

GET MOVING

This is the only time I condone manipulating people. A body in motion tends to stay in motion, so get yourself *and* your interrupter moving. They will be compelled to travel with you as you start moving, and when you have completed your task, you will have brought them to a physical location away from your work area where you can then safely leave them.

Announce that you'd like to get some water from the kitchen or take out the recycling and then go. Invite them to come with you and, as you're walking, address their issue and complete your task. When you're finished, be clear and direct by saying something like "I'm glad we had this chance to address X, and this is where I'll leave you. I'm now off to do Y. Have a great rest of your day!" And then briskly walk away without looking back.

ISOLATE YOURSELF

Almost everyone focuses better without noise or distraction, so find at least one place where you can isolate yourself for concentration when needed.

If you work from home, that may be a particular room or a quiet café or library off-site. If you work in an office, there may be privacy booths set up for this purpose, or you can get creative—maybe your building's lobby or even a nearby stairwell? You just need to know where you can go so no one can find you until you're ready to be found.

DON'T LEAVE ROOM FOR SQUATTERS

It's funny how easily you can subconsciously message the people around you in ways they won't consciously recognize. And this works equally well at home or at an office.

As you set up to work, pile things like papers, files, or other stuff on every free chair near you other than the one you are sitting in.

This will prevent anyone else from sitting down and getting comfortable. It is the rare person who will remove items to make themselves at home. This sends a subliminal message that there's "no room at the inn," so folks won't linger. It's a surefire way to limit people's interruptions and keep them on their toes, literally.

TURN OFF THOSE NOTIFICATIONS

Technology is a distraction, not an interruption, when *you* initiate its use. And I know it can be hard at first to build the habit of turning off your phone and putting it face down on your desk or other surface, but it will get easier quickly.

Of course, people will still call, text, and email you, and various apps will be waiting to alert you that you have new activity in some sector of your digital life, but you get to control when and how you respond.

You have the power and ability to silence your devices—really.

I already suggested you do this above, and if you thought I was joking, here's another chance to instantly change how often you are interrupted by machines.

So take a moment right now and turn off your notifications—or, even better, completely shut your devices down just because you can.

Modern cellphones can filter out all notifications except the truly urgent and important, like repeated phone calls from a family member or someone else in your contacts. So even though you are likely not a first responder, someone can still reach you in a true emergency.

JUGGLING COMPETING TASKS

Now let's return to anyone whose *actual job* is handling a steady stream of incoming phone calls or emails while also juggling administrative tasks.

If that does not describe your job, use this as a road map for how you can creatively pivot between the different kinds of tasks that make up your job. While the specifics may not apply, the problem-solving methodology does.

The best way to successfully manage different kinds of duties competing for your time and attention is to break down any task that does not involve other people into the smallest possible actions or steps so you can slot them in between tasks that do involve others.

For example, if your role involves immediate responses to customers and you're also tasked with creating reports, figure out the smallest increment of time it takes to do any single step of your reporting work and then book some of these "time chunks" into each day so you can pivot to them between calls or emails and keep track of your progress throughout the day.

If you're tasked with filing, you may have to file one document at a time. If you have to manage some correspondence, you may only have time to write one email or even one sentence at a time.

I understand this might seem burdensome or even a ridiculously small amount of time to dedicate to one task. At the same time, I can't change the structure of your job or your boss's expectations. You may be able to and we'll discuss that in a minute.

For now, what I can do is help you to manage your time as efficiently as possible and with the least amount of friction. If you are expected to shift between tasks that use different skills and different parts of your brain, you're going to need some way to isolate tasks and not lose your mind or waste a lot of time.

So you have nothing to lose other than some stress by experimenting with this way of chunking time.

And maybe as you experiment, your own ingenuity will unlock even better solutions to smoothly pivot between activities.

If you're feeling resistance to even attempting this, maybe your mindset could use a reframe? Any reflexive stories that come up about your job being "impossible" for anyone to do successfully, or about you being a "cog," or about management's disinterest in your happiness may be true.

But it might be just as true that no one has ever questioned your role's structure or raised these questions with management before, so they've never given this any attention.

The only thing you can know for sure is that until you ask, you're in your head and in a story.

BEING THE SQUEAKY WHEEL

If you aren't the first person in your role, you may just assume that the role was designed thoughtfully with your personal satisfaction and efficiency in mind, along with all the ways your role benefits the company's bottom line.

But jobs often evolve over time—based more on what a company needs and less on how that best uses the skills or impacts the happiness of whoever is sitting in a particular chair.

So here's your chance to be proactive and control what you can to be happier and more effective at work while also reducing your stress.

And if you're in management and you've seldom, if ever, considered the design of your direct reports' roles, here's your chance to step up, too.

Whether your manager expects it or not, you should make it a priority to investigate the overall structure of the organization and how it is contributing to workers' happiness or frustration.

Nothing has to remain as it is just because "that's how we've always done it," particularly if how you've always done it devalues workers and perpetuates a culture that allows or even rewards indiscriminate interruptions.

Because, deep down, everyone wants to feel valued and contribute to something bigger than themselves.

And if the structure where we work is benignly or actively undermining our ability to feel productive, the people who can leave, will—and the rest will stay and be miserable.

Their misery will impact their results and shape the culture much more than any motivational talks, trainings, or external interventions aimed at increasing productivity and efficiency will.

So if you want to avoid a slow, steady, and completely predictable race to the bottom, put an end to interruptions immediately.

THE BOTTOM LINE

The goal of any efficiency exercise is to improve productivity without increasing stress—if any solution doesn't involve both, it's not the right solution.

When you allow yourself to be interrupted, you are letting other people steal your time.

Putting boundaries in place lets you protect your concentration and maintain some degree of control over your own time and attention.

A culture at home or work that allows or even encourages interruptions shows a lack of respect for the individual's time, happiness, and productivity, and clearly communicates that any means to an end is acceptable.

So you are responsible for shifting any culture you're a part of that does that.

If you are in a supporting role, note all the ways interruptions interfere with your ability to concentrate and get your work done efficiently.

If you are in a leadership role, prioritize examining the existing culture for how it rewards interruptions.

Be a squeaky wheel and share personal anecdotal data as well as published data that quantifies the impact to morale and the other health and financial costs of a culture that ignores or encourages interruptions.

If we can help you in your pursuit of a more humane, responsive culture, write to us at hello@andrewmellen.com and we'll share additional strategies we've used for companies including American Express, Nationwide Insurance, and the New York Mets baseball team.

CHAPTER RECAP

Interruptions are the number one time thief. Finding a solution to them will revolutionize your productivity.

Without healthy and stable boundaries, you have zero control over your day. And the truth is that most interruptions can be anticipated or are not urgent, and your participation can wait.

When you stop interruptions, you build a firewall between you, your calendar, and everything else. It's the simplest and best way to protect your attention and energy so you can focus on the goals, tasks, and activities that matter most to you.

On average, we're interrupted by communications technology every 10 minutes. As we explored in Chapter 2, every interruption requires up to 23 minutes for recovery. That means that just 2 interruptions + 2 recoveries = up to 1 full hour of time lost.

The net time cost is even higher when you factor in the additional three interruptions that may happen every hour, along with any lost time from task switching and the time needed to regain your focus and resume your previous task.

Saying "no" or "not now" is the kindest and most direct way to protect your boundaries and show respect for other people's time. It also confirms your choices, since it allows you to stay focused on whatever you had already committed to and determined was important.

Interruptions and distractions are different animals. Interruptions are external—they happen outside of us. Distractions are internal—they are self-generated.

Interruptions show up as a ringing phone or a colleague stopping by your desk. Distractions look like you obsessively checking your phone, opening your email in the middle of a project to "switch things up," or scrolling absently through any app on your phone for the same reason.

HOW TO STOP OR REDUCE INTERRUPTIONS

The only way to stop interruptions is to shift the culture that allows or enables interruptions. At work and at home, make uninterrupted time an organizational or family priority, not a luxury or an indulgence.

Remember that change is always possible. Nothing has to remain as it is just because "that's how we've always done it," particularly if how you've always done it perpetuates a culture that allows or even rewards interruptions.

As you work to change the culture, these techniques will minimize the impact of any interruptions as they occur:

- Make constraints known. When someone interrupts you and your tasking, set a timer for an agreed-upon duration; then, when the timer goes off, excuse the other person and return to your previous task.
- Run an errand and invite the interrupter to accompany you. When you reach your destination, announce that you will now continue solo and they are free to return to whatever they need to do next.
- Group all online activities together. You're less likely to be interrupted or snagged by popups, etc., when you're online if you go online fewer times and with greater focus. So instead of hopping on and off throughout your day, go online strategically, do what needs to be done, and then get offline ASAP. Close down your browser to prevent additional notifications from showing up.
- Isolate yourself for concentration. Put yourself someplace where you likely won't be found. That way, you can work for as long as you want beyond reach. It may mean leaving where you were for a café, library, the inside of your car,

or even a stairwell, as long as you're comfortable enough to concentrate on your task(s) while there.

- Keep something on any available chair near you. If every seating option nearby is already filled with things stacked on it, when someone interrupts you they are less likely to linger if they can't sit down themselves.

To get things moving even faster, follow these steps:

1. Turn off all notifications immediately.
2. Identify your distractions and interruptions at home and work:

   a. Go to cbobbook.com/interruptions, download the Interruptions Worksheet, and fill it out.
   b. For one week, record any additional interruptions and distractions as they happen.
   c. To strategize how you will minimize or eliminate each interruption you've listed, use your timer and begin brainstorming all the ways you could stop it from occurring again.

3. Take action on the strategies you brainstormed in Step 2. If none of them work, go back to 2(c) and try again.

Chapter 5

Multitasking

"Multitasking? I can't do two things at once.
I can't even do one thing at once."
Helena Bonham Carter

Multitasking is impossible. You may be arguing in your head right now that not only is multitasking *not* impossible, it is in fact your superpower. If so, that is definitely one of your 200 lies.

You can't bake a cake and perform open-heart surgery at the exact same time.

Which isn't to deny the appeal behind the lie.

If you could save time by doing two or more things at once—like checking email while you're in a meeting, or coding a website while you're walking the dog—it would be an incredible time-saver.

But if you've ever glanced away from the road while driving and then looked up just in time to see the car in front of you screeching to a halt, you know that you can't effectively focus on two things at once.

You might *think* that you're still aware of what's going on in front of you while you glance away, but that's not what's happening in your brain. You're not multitasking; you're rapidly switching between tasks.

Think of your focus as a spotlight. That spotlight can only shine on one fixed area at any given time. When you think you're "multitasking," you're actually swinging that spotlight back and forth, not lighting up two different areas simultaneously.

Even if you're swinging it very fast, it's still swinging.

And this is what we know about swinging your spotlight or, more accurately, task switching. Studies repeatedly show that constantly switching tasks—and, as a result, your focus—comes at a cost.[25]

Let's look at the example of checking your email in a meeting. You're either paying attention to the meeting or reading your email. When you're listening to the speaker in the meeting, how carefully are you reading your emails? And if you're deep in your inbox, how much of the meeting are you really taking in?

When you attempt to multitask, you're failing at two things at once. You do both tasks less well—and often, you have to go back and do them again.

And the reality is, if you did just one of those things at any given time, you'd be *more* efficient—not less. Studies show that we consistently overestimate our ability to multitask.[26] Focusing on one task at a time enables us to give that task our full attention.

Our work and our relationships both improve when we are fully present for the task at hand. We invest less time in the long run *and* get better results.

THE HARD COSTS OF MULTITASKING

Regardless of how stubborn you are and how strongly you want to cling to some of your 200 lies, consider these problems with and consequences of multitasking:

YOU'LL DO YOUR TASK LESS WELL

When you're not paying full attention to a task, you're more likely to make errors, especially avoidable errors. From distracted driving to sloppy emails, the data proves this—we make stupid, and sometimes fatal, mistakes when our attention is elsewhere.[27]

YOUR TASK WILL TAKE LONGER IN SEVERAL WAYS

- The time costs from task switching have been the subject of multiple studies. This was covered in Chapter 4 as well. Every time you redirect your spotlight of focus to something else, you lose valuable time and momentum because it takes time for your brain to shift gears and refocus on its new object.
- Correcting the mistakes you make when jumping from one task to another eats up time, which is seldom budgeted for. Take emails, for example. Instead of sending one focused, comprehensive email, you may end up sending multiple clarifying messages back and forth. Or you may have to resend corrected emails due to typos, wrong information, omissions, or additions. And in the context of a bigger project, one small mistake could create huge problems down the line. The more complex and expensive the project, the more your mistakes cost.

YOU WILL DESTROY YOUR ABILITY TO FOCUS

When you attempt to multitask, you are actively training your brain to *not* focus on whatever you're doing at that moment. The longer you "practice" multitasking, the harder it becomes to focus on a single task.

You are also undermining any benefits you might have gleaned from mindfulness training or a meditation practice where single-minded focus is a primary objective.

YOU'LL WASTE YOUR MONEY—AND EVERYONE ELSE'S

First, there's the additional time spent both executing and correcting mistakes as outlined above. That's money. Then your mistakes and delays may require additional time from others—more money.

And what if any of those mistakes involve tangible assets, like buying things you don't need, breaking or losing things while distracted, or overlooking recurring or duplicate charges for things you don't need or want? There are lots of ways that multitasking failures cost money.

You may try to discount these costs by framing them as "on the company's dime," but that would be both irresponsible and wrong. No company can survive that degree of waste for long. Whether it's your company or you're "just" an employee, when the business fails or fires you, what will you do for income?

TIME IS A NONRENEWABLE RESOURCE

It's the one thing you can never get back—money can be earned, but you'll never regain the time you've spent, whether it was invested well or wasted.

So you can tell yourself stories about 5 minutes here and 10 minutes there, as if that time were negligible, but the truth is that the average person will waste one year of their life looking for lost or misplaced items . . . and if you add the time wasted redoing distracted or sloppy work, you can easily see and feel how those costs compound.

Do you want to spend your time cleaning up avoidable messes, or would you rather be doing something you love?

MULTITASKING CAN BE DANGEROUS

Most of us will be in an automobile at some time in our lives.

Here's the math of texting and driving—sending or reading even a short text takes your eyes off the road for an average of five seconds. At 55 mph, you would cover 403 feet in that time—that's longer than a US football field. Worst of all, the average accident occurs in just under three seconds.[28]

Less fatal but not less dangerous are accidents in the kitchen.

If you've ever hurt yourself while cooking, you know why some health and safety experts consider the kitchen to be the most dangerous room in the house. And they all agree that most mishaps are the result of either rushing or multitasking.

Then there's daily work in dangerous environments like construction sites, laboratories, and manufacturing facilities, where a distracted moment can also have fatal consequences.

YOUR LONG-TERM BRAIN HEALTH WILL SUFFER

Multitasking is managed by executive functions in the brain designed to control cognitive processes and determine the relative priority and order of tasks.

That means every time you rapidly shift between tasks, you make your brain work harder, and not in a good way. It had just sorted everything you were thinking about. Now it has to consider what new thing you're asking it to do, evaluate its significance, then reprioritize everything it was doing, factoring in the new task as well.

So, while the amount of energy this takes each time is small, multiplied over dozens or hundreds of times a day, the increased energy demands are huge.

Remember, your brain is designed to keep you safe and then rest—keeping it in a constant state of alert is like driving down the road with your emergency brake on. You may get the car to move, but it will be burning through parts and fuel super quick and super hot.

The more you encourage your brain to bounce around between tasks, the more you destroy its ability to sustain peak performance for any length of time.

WHY IT MATTERS

If you're folding laundry and watching TV at the same time, the stakes for impairing either task are pretty low. Maybe you end up with some mismatched socks or lose a key plot twist in your favorite TV show—but the quality of your life probably won't suffer too much.

But like most habits, the more you do it, the more you do it. And if low-level multitasking without major consequences encourages more involved multitasking, it's only a matter of time before someone is texting and driving—except you're not texting *and* driving; you're texting *or* driving.

Which is why texting is six times more likely to cause an accident than driving drunk.[29]

This experiment by Christopher Chabris and Daniel Simons also illustrates this point.

Go to the video link in the endnotes and follow the on-screen prompts.[30] Don't read any of the associated text on the page. You'll be asked to watch a video of people passing a basketball back and forth, and to count the number of passes.

If you were focused on counting the number of passes, odds are you missed the gorilla walking through—that's the kind of thing our brain filters out when something appears and is out of sync with the task we're already focused on.

The Institute of Psychiatry did a study at the University of London with 1,100 workers multitasking with electronic media. They found that when the workers were rapidly switching between electronic devices, they experienced a greater decrease in IQ than someone who had not slept in 24 hours or who was under the influence of marijuana.[31]

If you're like the average participant in that study, your "story" about multitasking says you're firing on all cylinders as you juggle multiple devices.

The scientific proof is that you are less effective than someone who just pulled an all-nighter or who is high on pot. Fiction, meet reality.

It's also helpful to note that when you focus on just one task at a time, your productivity skyrockets—by a whopping 40 percent.[32]

So unlearn one bad habit—multitasking— and you can increase your productivity by 40 percent instantly.

HOW TO STOP MULTITASKING

Or attempting to multitask, since we now know that you can't multitask.

Start by slowing down just enough to complete one task at a time, and then smoothly pivot to the next task.

When you set something down and turn your attention in another direction, you want that transition to be quick but not rushed.

You also don't want to be snagged by unfinished business or lingering thoughts about your previous task. That's why using a timer to define how long you'll put your attention somewhere is so important.

When you think you have to finish the task to stop working on it, it's hard to step away cleanly in midstream—partly because you are thinking of it as midstream.

If, instead, you use a timer to specify when you're finished, when that timer goes off, you *are* finished.

Doing this repeatedly trains us that focused work for a defined time *is* the task—the only goal is working uninterrupted for the entire duration.

With a greater sense of success and less attachment to another outcome, your transition between tasks can flow almost like a martial art or walking meditation.

The transition becomes about precision, fluidity of movement, and conserving energy. It should take you only what is required to pivot, nothing extra.

In meditation practice, the concept of shoshin or "beginner's mind" refers to seeing things with an open mind, without expectations or preconceived ideas about something. It's about leaning into your curiosity instead of your judgment.

While adopting that point of view is useful anywhere in our lives, it's particularly helpful here as you try to learn a few things and unlearn a few others.

Let go of trying to do two things at once. Let the timer define "finished" for you instead of a specific outcome. And practice setting down one task and transitioning to another task smoothly, without any sticky residue or hesitation.

You'll gain proficiency as you practice. Your beginner's mind will help you release any expectations or perfectionism.

The more you can just "be" and "do" your pivots, observing without judging, the simpler they will become, until you can easily swivel between activities without friction.

If you notice that as you're pivoting you're getting sidetracked or snagged on something—a bit of story, a previous or upcoming task, one of your 200 lies—just call it out, write it down if necessary, and let it go.

Then refocus on the next task with renewed energy, clarity, and intention.

It will take practice to let go of wanting to do more than one thing at a time and to stay focused in the present moment.

You may be unlearning a long history of trying to multitask, and it may be unfamiliar to just be here, now.

The good news is that it really is as simple as that—simple, but not always easy.

Here are some tools to help.

PRACTICE FOCUS INTERVALS

Think of these almost like split training in the gym. In this case, you're going to flex a particular set of mental muscles for a set period of time. You're not exercising *all* muscles, just some, and for a defined quantity of time.

To start, turn off all notifications and set a timer. The amount of time isn't as important as the timer itself, so start with a period that seems easy and doable. The point is relying on the timer rather than your mind to manage your time.

If you can only focus for five minutes to start, go with five minutes. For those five minutes, focus on just one task. If you're distracted, just come back to the task at hand. It's a loving way of correcting a fidgety mind until it settles down and digs in.

Eventually, you'll build your focus muscle so that it's strong enough to work for longer periods: 15 minutes, 25 minutes, even an hour without interruptions or looking around for something to distract you.

You'll find very quickly that you get significantly better results when you dedicate your full attention to a single task.

CLARIFY YOUR PRIORITIES

Time thieves like multitasking sneak in when you aren't sure what needs to be done at the moment or you're feeling overwhelmed and want some relief. Trying to get a few things done at the same time can seem like a logical way to treat your anxiety or agitation.

But the best antidote to anxiety or overwhelm is planning. And while we'll dive deeper into that in Chapter 7, let's look at your calendar to focus on what needs to be done next.

What's on your schedule for today? Are there things on the calendar that aren't so important?

Don't discount your intuition that something isn't worth your time. Bounce it off your values for confirmation if needed.

If they don't need to be done today, reschedule them for another day. Are there things that *are* important and should be addressed today? Maybe move them into your now freed-up time slots.

When *why* you're doing what you're doing is aligned with your values, it's easier to stay focused and not get distracted—and easier to prioritize.

KEEP YOUR SPACES CLEAN AND ORGANIZED

Cleaning or tidying up your workspace is a tempting multitasking activity. And I'm all for order and cleanliness. Tidying up during a call—especially one where video isn't required—may seem harmless. But if you truly need to be on that call, you probably also need to be paying attention.

If you don't need to be on the call, why are you? That's not a rhetorical question. If you don't know the answer, you're liable to keep burning through your time as if it's a renewable resource, which it isn't.

Either be all in on the call or get off the call and do something of greater value . . . like putting your stuff away quickly and without distraction.

THE BOTTOM LINE

The ability to pivot cleanly between focused tasks is a strength. And developing that strength is well within your grasp.

Your agency and ability to self-direct your life belongs to you—it's your birthright as a human being. You can attribute it to a god of your understanding or a higher power or just the nature of being an apex mammal on the planet—whatever you believe, you get to determine how you spend each minute of this finite existence.

As with interruptions, when you assert your right and ability to focus, you are telling the world at large, and yourself, "I know what's important to me, what I have to do, what I want to do, and I'm going to do that now."

Attempting to do more than one task at a time shows poor judgment and indecision, and it's not your superpower—it's a weakness and not the good kind of vulnerability.

As soon as you try to juggle that second task, you cut your productivity by 40 percent. Instantly. And you've created an opportunity for disaster.

I'm guessing *that* is not listed on your resumé as one of your strengths.

Using the timer, build your "concentration muscle" by gradually increasing the time you can stay focused and productive.

If you find your mind wandering or reaching for something to speed up the process or add some spice to what you're doing, stop tasking and don't start again until you've decided which is more important— what you were doing or what you're now thinking about doing. Then reset your timer and start working on the task you've now prioritized.

CHAPTER RECAP

Multitasking is *not* your superpower. Not only that—it's impossible. You can't bake a cake and perform open heart surgery simultaneously. Even talking on the phone while doing the dishes is not actually multitasking—you are just rapidly switching your attention between tasks, not doing two things at the exact same time.

Imagine your focus as a spotlight. It can only shine on one fixed area at a time. When you think you're multitasking, you're actually swinging that spotlight back and forth very quickly, not lighting up two different areas simultaneously. Many scientific studies have documented this.

The good news is that doing one thing at a time makes you more efficient—not less. As soon as you stop fracturing your focus, you instantly increase your productivity by up to 40 percent.

HOW TO STOP MULTITASKING

Once you accept that staying focused on one thing at a time is superior to trying to get better at an impossibility, as seductive as it has seemed in the past, you can use these tips to build your focus muscle:

- Use a timer and practice working in focused intervals—set periods of time when you will do one task and nothing else. When the timer goes off, you are finished. Doing this repeatedly trains you that focused work for a defined time is the task—the only goal is working uninterrupted for the entire duration.
- Practice an interval right now. Identify your starting focus interval length. If you aren't sure where to start, try five minutes. If five is too long, try two. Don't judge yourself for how long you can stay focused—you will build your endurance over time. For now, just do what you can do and proceed from there. Set your timer now and focus on one

task exclusively, which could be reading the rest of this chapter recap.

- Whenever the timer goes off, take a few seconds and observe what you accomplished. Pay particular attention to how often you were tempted to switch focus to something else. You can also note what you did or said to yourself to resist switching.

- To gamify the experience even more, you can tally those distracted moments and then track the number of times you almost leave tasks for something else over a seven-day period. If this would not be fun, don't do it. No data gathering or the data you gather should be used to beat up on or shame yourself.

- Get clear on your priorities—on what you want to do, have to do, and in what order. When you know what you need to accomplish, it's easier to stay on task and work your way through your day as scheduled in your calendar.

- Keep your space clean and neat. Clutter can distract you. And your desire for a tidy space can trick you into thinking you can clean your office while on a conference call, but you can't. Not well, anyway.

Chapter 6
Overcommitting

"You wouldn't worry so much about what others think
of you if you realized how seldom they do."
Eleanor Roosevelt

"When you work so hard to get everyone to like you,
you very often end up not liking yourself so much."
Reshma Saujani

If you've ever thought of yourself as a people pleaser, this chapter is going to change your life in ways that you can't even imagine yet . . . Woo hoo!

Whether or not this label describes you, these are some of the ways that overcommitting might show up in your day-to-day behavior:

- Double-booking appointments
- Volunteering for things before you check in with your gut or your calendar
- Saying yes because you were flattered to even be asked
- Saying yes because of a promise of riches, fame, glory, or all three
- Saying yes while discounting how taking on another commitment will impact existing obligations
- Indulging in self-talk such as "This is too X, Y, or Z to pass up!" or "I just have a ton of interests!"

- Indulging in self-talk such as "I'll rest/sleep when I'm dead!"
- Dissociating, and when you come to, feeling like a passenger or a hostage in your own life
- Wearing "running yourself ragged" as a badge of honor and proof of your commitment, stamina, and/or passion
- Getting to the end of your day exhausted with no time left for yourself
- Having to choose between meeting your obligations and even the minimum of self-care
- Staying up so late that you sabotage tomorrow's pacing or success
- Resenting other people or organizations even while performing tasks or projects for them

If any of that sounds familiar, you're probably falling prey to this time thief.

People who hate conflict in their own relationships are especially vulnerable to this thief, even when they are fierce advocates for others' boundaries.

And there are plenty of reasons for this.

For one thing, it's nice to feel needed. Most of us get an ego boost from having others rely on us or being the go-to resource for help and guidance, right?

Not surprisingly, this can happen at work or at home—it's equally problematic wherever it occurs.

Unfortunately, overcommitting can quickly poison your relationships from the inside out. It's so easy to grow resentful of the people you love or care about when you feel like they are taking advantage of you— even though *you* may have volunteered or encouraged them to do it.

Saying yes to things and making others happy aren't inherently bad choices, of course.

But when you do either without carefully considering all the implications of your choices, you can easily create the very sense of overwhelm you probably picked up this book to address.

When it comes to your commitments, remember this: you have chosen everything that you said yes and no to.

It might *feel* like you didn't have a choice, as when you're caring for an ailing family member or taking on extra work that your boss is throwing at you. But even in those situations, you do have agency. You *can* say no.

You might not like the consequences of saying no, but that is what you're actually choosing between—the consequences of saying yes and the consequences of saying no.

In situations where it feels impossible to refuse, like providing health care to a family member, you still need to actively choose to take on the responsibility or it may quickly devolve into something icky and imposing.

If you take on any commitment while feeling powerless, you're priming the pump for resentment. By retaining your sense of power, even when making the best of a crappy situation, you feel like you are still at the helm—because you are.

That's why it's also important to leverage your values and long-range goals when making these kinds of decisions. Any negative consequences of saying yes will be easier to accept when viewed through the lens of your values and goals.

These simple adjustments have huge long-term benefits for our mental health.

Now, back to saying yes—it feels good to say yes, right?

Humans love to feel pleasure, and you can get a hit of dopamine (a pleasure-reward neurotransmitter) from anything as small as agreeing to type up a call sheet for the PTA to volunteering to host a fancy fundraiser—primarily when the ask or opportunity is unexpected.

Brain science tells us that once we come to expect a result, the dopamine levels actually decrease.[33] So we get our biggest hits when we're pleasantly surprised—that's why volunteering or being chosen feels so good.

When we chase that rush too often, though, we can find ourselves out of control of our own time. We're busy juggling everyone else's priorities ahead of our own, and racing headlong into burnout.

At that point, it may be hard to remember why we first raised our hand or agreed to do something.

Owning the choice of saying yes starts with accepting that everything you say yes to means you are simultaneously saying no to something else.

And the end of that choice only comes when either your commitment is completed or you renege on your promise.

THE PROBLEMS WITH OVERCOMMITTING

Most of us can remember a time when we indulged in a knee-jerk "yes" and then had to go back on our word. It feels crappy, right?

The fallout from an early exit can follow you for years, if not your entire life. You may forget it over time—others may hold a grudge forever.

For some of us, overcommitting can also become an addiction if we aren't careful.

Here's how Dr. Judson Brewer, author of *Unwinding Anxiety*, defines an addiction: "continued use despite adverse consequences."[34] So, yes, literally an addiction.

As with other addictions, your brain can start to crave the feel-good dopamine jolt of taking on extra work or agreeing to do someone a favor, and so you compulsively seek out new ways to say yes.

And because of an addict's built-in "forgetter," you may minimize or dismiss the negative consequences that arise, focusing only on the next rush. The lies and half-truths pile up as you try to convince yourself that you can still manage your schedule. Even as the pattern repeats itself, you swear, with no proof, that this time will be different.

Can you see how insidious this time thief can be? Only procrastination offers a similar reward on the front end.

Beyond creating a chemical dependency in your brain, overcommitting causes lots of other problems. Here are a few of them.

YOU'LL CONSTANTLY RUN OUT OF TIME

We all get the same 24 hours a day, 7 days a week. You only have so much space in your time buckets—and if you're filling them up with other people's priorities, there will be little room left for what matters to you.

And if you haven't discovered this yet, here's some sobering news— there will never be "enough time" to do everything in the world. Sorry.

It's also unlikely you'll run out of things to do, reaching a time when you're all caught up, nothing is looming or waiting for you, and you've got a straight path on to your next big project.

So the more you reach for, the more aggressive your schedule will be, and you won't just feel like you don't have any time—you won't.

YOU'LL USE ANYTHING TO AVOID QUIET TIME ALONE

An empty surface can freak some people out so much that they feel the need to "decorate" it with tchotchkes and other visual noise. If quiet unstructured time bothers you the same way, you may find yourself cramming things into your day to avoid spending any time alone. Sometimes you'll grab onto activities you have no interest in just to stay busy.

If that has been true in the past, please consider developing the ability to sit still and be with yourself. You don't need to become a Buddhist monk meditating silently for hours to enjoy the many benefits of a few unstructured minutes of meditation or quiet reflection.

Sitting in nature or even staring out the window at a peaceful landscape can also quiet down your mind and reduce stress.

You may be surprised to learn that these benefits are similar to the ones you get during a brainstorm or "lightbulb" moment alone in the shower.

YOU'LL FREQUENTLY SHOW UP UNPREPARED

When you're rushing from one thing to the next, with no breathing room in between, you're inevitably going to show up unprepared for something and then be forced to wing it.

A further complication is that you may not know what you're unprepared for until you arrive—like the actor's nightmare of finding yourself on stage performing in a play you've never rehearsed before.

Racing from thing to thing, it will be hard to prioritize. Whatever you're running toward is likely to get your attention, regardless of how important it is compared with other tasks.

To save face, you may also try to button up one last thing on whatever you were just doing, and that effort may be a bit scattered and random, too.

When your schedule is packed this tightly, you may only have enough time to put your head down, plow through, and task. So even if you wanted to prepare in advance, there aren't enough hours in the day.

YOU'LL BURN OUT AND RECOVER MORE SLOWLY

Keeping yourself running on that hamster wheel of revolving tasks means that there's no time to rest or recharge.

Sadly, your smartphone is quite a bit smarter than you; if it was running at the pace you are, it would shut down and just refuse to work until it was recharged. You, on the other hand, forge ahead, ignoring internal warning lights and alarms until you collapse. The phone just needs a few minutes to be up and running again. You may need medical intervention—seriously.

Returning to the idea of addiction, when you're operating at this pitch, you are also likely dismissing previous consequences from similar behavior. "This time will be different," your 200 lies tell you, and like a true junkie, you believe it.

YOU'LL BE MENTALLY ABSENT . . . POSSIBLY A LOT

Whenever we talk about being present, we mean physically present and mentally present, too.

When you're wrapped up in thoughts about the past or worries about the future, you can't be where you are in the moment.

Now, if you're attending a meeting that has nothing to offer you, it's understandable that your mind would wander.

In those cases, it would be better to excuse yourself and go do something else rather than waste time somewhere you don't belong.

When you're exhausted, you may find yourself someplace you *do* want to be, but you're too tired to be there mentally.

What a shame to miss your child's wedding, their winning goal, or even your own special events by being there physically, yet completely checked out inside your head.

YOU'LL GROW CRANKIER AND MORE RESENTFUL

Everyone has a bad day and, occasionally, even a string of them . . . but when every day sucks, it's probably not the day but your attitude, right?

The irony, of course, is that for many people, much of our misery is our own doing.

If you're so busy that you can't see straight, and you're cramming so many things into your life that you're starting to resent the people and experiences you love, what are you doing to yourself?

And to the people you say you love?

When you spend more time apologizing for being a jerk than smiling and laughing with your peeps, you've crossed a line.

Hopefully you can still see the line before it turns into a dot behind you and the only thing ahead is a burned-out bridge.

MORE CONSEQUENCES OF OVERCOMMITTING

We've already discussed some of the consequences of this voracious time thief. They are compounded by the fact that overcommitting is a social time thief, meaning it involves other people.

That is one reason why its hold on us can be so strong and why it's harder to shut this thief down.

Saying no to activities, commitments, and invitations can be viewed as saying no to or rejecting other people, instead of just the event.

Of course, anyone who takes "no" personally could probably use better boundaries, too.

In don Miguel Ruiz's book, *The Four Agreements,* we learn to take nothing personally. This agreement has proved very helpful in my own life. We also use it as a guiding principle in all of our online programs.

One of the reasons many people struggle with clutter is that they take things personally—and value the story behind an object more than they value their own well-being.

For those of us programmed to put others first, focusing on ourselves often kicks up feelings of shame and starts a stream of negative self-talk accusing us of being selfish.

It is helpful to figure out whose voice that is . . . because it's almost never our own.

In my case, I can draw a direct line back to a few adult family members in my life. They meant well and were worried that, as an only child, I might grow up spoiled and lacking empathy.

Unfortunately, their own narcissistic tendencies clouded a legitimate concern and fueled their criticism.

So any attempt to assert myself and my needs, if they were at odds with these adults', would trigger a warning of selfishness.

I was a curious and willful child, so I heard that warning a lot.

As a result, it took a long time to learn and understand that, just because I want something that you may not want, my happiness does not threaten your happiness—particularly when it's pursued ethically and honestly.

If you have had similar experiences in your past, it may take a lot of effort for you, too, to assert yourself and effectively protect your time.

Disappointing others should not be the primary factor in making your choices—disappointing yourself should be.

Another consequence of overcommitting may be that the quality of your work starts to suffer.

There will be times when you have to choose between doing something well and just doing it at all. Has this already happened to you?

When there is too much to do and not enough time to do it all, something has to give. And that might mean redefining what you consider to be "good enough," let alone "excellent."

When your standards start slipping and you're unwilling to accept that, you set up a pattern of unrealistic expectations followed by disappointment and shame. And the consequences of that pattern include chronic stress, anxiety, depression, and even suicide.[35]

GETTING GOOD AT SAYING NO

If you want to be happy and successful, you're going to have to get good at saying no.

We humans are social creatures and most of us have a built-in and inherent distaste for conflict—so we don't want to let other people down or, worse, make them angry with us.

Given that, it may seem like being agreeable has a net benefit socially, but pushing back at the right moment is actually better for ourselves and others.

Remember the airline instruction to put on your own oxygen mask before helping others? That rule applies here, too.

You can't show up for others when you're overreaching, because often you're not actually present enough to do so. And when you're rapidly approaching burnout, you're pretty useless to everyone, including yourself.

Also, I'm not a doctor, but you don't need an MD to tell you that stress and anxiety take a very heavy toll on your health over time.

So the simplest way to take care of yourself is to knock off the people pleasing and overcommitting now.

And don't just agree to do it because you don't want to upset me. *That would be more people pleasing* . . .

Do it because you want to be happy, healthy, and actually useful when you agree to take care of others.

HOW TO STOP OVERCOMMITTING

When you think of your life, do you feel trapped and at the mercy of forces outside of your control?

If so, take a moment and imagine how you'd feel if you and your values were controlling your schedule, and it moved at a human pace.

What if, when you looked at your calendar, instead of seeing conflicting and competing appointments all day, you saw empty spaces where you had the flexibility to use that time for recharging or reflecting?

To move from the first scenario to the second, you have to accept the premise that you are not indispensable, no matter how good you are at what you do.

Often, we consciously or unconsciously engineer things to reinforce the feeling and appearance that we are essential—and while that may be true on a spiritual level, it's seldom true in the most literal sense.

It's one of the reasons why we fail to document processes or teach others how to do repetitive tasks that we might easily outsource. If we reveal our "secret sauce," we might get replaced.

And when we get praised for jumping in and doing the work of two people, our subconscious laps it up and de-incentivizes us to let those tasks go—even when the work could be redistributed back to the role you were temporarily covering.

Of course, all of this madness can only go on so long. Eventually, we'll take on so much that we can't keep all those plates spinning, and either they fall and break or we crash and burn . . . or both.

You don't have to stop saying yes cold turkey, but you'll see the fastest results if you do. Either way, here's how to wean yourself away from overcommitting.

TAKE CONTROL OF YOUR CALENDAR

If you aren't currently driving your day *from* your calendar, please start. Then stop indulging the lie that says everything would be fine if you could only stop the external demands on your time.

Even if you are literally in prison, you may still have some control over how your day goes.

And for the rest of us who are not behind bars, whether we're struggling with serious poverty, active addictions, other institutional structures, or social injustices, we have to claim as much of our time as we can. Because no one is ever going to have a greater stake in our well-being or happiness than we are—no one.

And if you don't have any of those additional demands on your attention and energy, you've already won the time lottery. So stop any complaining and take ownership of your obligations and commitments now.

Take responsibility for everything that is happening in your life. Blame is useless, and you're looking in the wrong direction if you're looking outward for any relief from the demands on your time.

The quickest way out of this cycle is to either complete everything you've already committed to or let some things go and then immediately stop the problem behaviors—that is, overcommitting and people pleasing.

REFINE YOUR ABILITY TO PRIORITIZE

What are your level-1, -2, and -3 priorities—and what are the 4s and 5s?

High-priority tasks like 1s and 2s should always come first when you're prioritizing, followed by 3s to fill in the gaps. Levels 4 and 5 should *never* be on your calendar—give these away or delete them. We already talked about your golf balls in Chapter 1, and we'll cover this in greater detail in Chapter 7.

Now, if you work for a boss who has no concept of time and throws way too much at you every day, you still have a voice and can ask that boss for help prioritizing.

If their response is, "Figure it out, that's what I'm paying you for," then, with love, I think you need to find a different boss. That response sucks.

If you can go around them or above them to get support in effectively prioritizing, you should. And if the culture where you work is so toxic that everyone in management has the same shitty attitude, really, the business deserves to fail and you deserve a job where your intelligence, commitment, and abilities are honored.

I realize how easy it is for me to say this. Still, you deserve to work someplace where you are valued. So please consider what you need to do to take care of yourself and break free from a work environment that will never support your health or happiness.

Barring the nightmare described above . . .

START SAYING NO . . . AND MEANING IT

Remember, every time you say yes to something new, you're saying no to something else—either something you've already committed to or something that hasn't shown up yet.

It helps if you think of your calendar as a plate and life like a buffet. You can load your plate up with everything from the start, but then you have to eat it all, right?

Or you could walk through the whole buffet first and then decide where you want to start.

In the first scenario, you may end up with a bunch of pasta before you see they also have crab cakes.

So then you have to either throw away the pasta, which is wasteful, or eat it anyway, overstuffing yourself before you even get to the crab cakes.

It could be enough to appreciate all the different choices without having to pile them on top of each other until your plate is packed, just because you can.

This is the same advice I give people around clutter and shopping. It can be enough to just enjoy seeing things in stores without having to buy them all and bring them home.

This is another reference to the story about golf balls, pebbles, and sand from Chapter 1. Once you've decided what your golf balls are, schedule them first.

When other requests come in, you can weigh them against your golf balls. Is the new item something you value more than the existing balls? If not, it's an easy no. You simply don't have the time.

WAIT 24 HOURS BEFORE SAYING YES

Develop the practice of saying, "Thank you for the offer. It sounds great. I just need 24 hours to check my calendar and prior commitments before I say yes." And then stop talking.

While you'll give up the sudden thrill of rushing into something, you'll save yourself a lot of trouble and heartache when you have to say no later *or* force yourself to do something you don't want to do or even have enough time for.

LEVERAGE YOUR VALUES WHEN DECIDING WHAT TO TAKE ON

It may sound silly or self-evident, but take a few seconds to decide whether you *want* to do something before you agree to it. When we're in the habit of saying yes without thinking the choice through, it stops being a choice—it's just a reflexive reaction.

So start practicing the simple act of deciding whether the thing you're agreeing to belongs on your calendar or to-do list at all.

Availability shouldn't be the only criterion for the invitations and requests you accept. If you have the time but not the desire, the answer should still be no.

It's always a good idea to maintain some free time on your calendar for high-value or fun, spontaneous things that will pop up later.

LEARN TO DELEGATE

If there aren't enough hours in the day to get everything done, there are only two ways to free up time for yourself: drop some tasks or outsource them.

There are many freelance labor apps and other sources for hiring help with all kinds of things—from running errands to renovating your bathroom.

So, whether you need a virtual assistant online or someone to deliver groceries locally, every day there are more options available to get things done without *you* having to do them.

Outsourcing small tasks can be less expensive than you'd think—and when you factor in the value of the time you're saving, the investment may be worth more than just the money if it helps you clear out some space on your calendar.

If you don't have the funds to hire help, apps like Nextdoor offer boards where neighbors volunteer to pitch in. If you're not too proud to accept help, it may be available for free. I've seen many posts from local people offering to pick up groceries, walk pets, or collect kids from school. We've already identified that it feels good to help . . . *so let someone else enjoy giving, too.*

You could also look closer to home and consider delegating (or redistributing) tasks among your partner, kids, and other family members.

I'm still amazed at how many women are tasked with the bulk of the housework and child care while working every bit as hard and long at a paid job as their male partners—what's up with that?

Above all, be honest with yourself about whether you've consciously or unconsciously taken on this much because you love how it feels to "do it all."

DON'T OVERPACK YOUR CALENDAR

I know we live in a culture where more is more and social media deliberately feeds your worst FOMO nightmares. You can disconnect from that noise at any time and make choices that resonate with you.

If you've been told that you *can* have it all, you've been lied to—if what's implied is that you can have it all simultaneously. Depending on what you consider "all" to be, you may be able to have it all . . . over time. But probably not without some help.

So, with that in mind, your calendar should *not* be packed full.

A full calendar is a recipe for failure, exhaustion, guilt, shame, or worse—because few things go exactly according to plan and you're not a robot.

Last-minute tasks and complications will come up that you can't foresee, and when they do, you'll have to pivot and let other stuff drop or wait to be handled. Additional problems may occur if you don't quickly reschedule those now-delayed tasks . . . so don't make that mistake.

Not taking this one step creates a backlog that haunts many people. Starting today, don't let that be you.

You also can't maintain a pace that has you moving from task to task with no breaks or breathing room—it's not sustainable.

FOMO is a shitty excuse for busy-ness, too. Whatever your hyper-competitive neighbor, sibling, high school crush, or frenemy is doing that looks amazing on Instagram, social media is the real fake news.

Unless you are committed to being miserable, stop comparing your life to anyone else's—especially on social sites that run on algorithms designed to feed your anxiety.

Include some buffers in your schedule so you don't burn out and can pivot smoothly and without friction between activities.

These buffers also leave some room for spontaneity and other opportunities. Sometimes great stuff falls into your lap and you can slot it into these blank spaces—but you won't be able to if you don't leave any room for life to surprise you.

TREAT "NO" AS A COMPLETE SENTENCE
Put an end to the habit of defending your choices and, more important, feeling like you have to defend them.

Catch yourself every time you say "because" and pay attention to what you are saying and why you are saying it.

Few people will challenge you when you say no. And you don't need a "better" reason for declining—because *you don't want to* is a good-enough reason.

Explanations when not required keep you off-balance and feeling defensive—and more focused on how your "no" is being received than feeling grounded in your choice.

It's okay to say no and then be quiet.

Of course, saying no doesn't have to be aggressively blunt or rude, or give you permission to be a dick, either—so if it's new to you, watch that you don't overcorrect the first few times you stand up for yourself.

You can simply say something like "Thank you for asking, but I won't be able to attend/participate/do X."

Build this muscle until you're comfortable saying no without explaining first. Otherwise, you leave the door open for others to weasel their way into your head and heart, then manipulate you into going back on your decision.

Some bosses are especially good at the weasel dance—see the points above about prioritizing.

And when it comes to work especially, there is a difference between saying "no" and saying "not now."

So, if you are asked to take on additional work for no extra pay, it's good to have a response already rehearsed.

If anyone tries to play on your fear or pride by implying that someone else could handle the task just fine, you could say, "While I'm a team player, I know that so-and-so was getting X for doing this task as part of their job and it's outside the current scope of my role."

Or you might say, "I'm happy to take on this new responsibility and I'll need your help in deciding what I should now deprioritize or delegate in order to make space for this new task."

As a result, one of three things may happen:

- You may get an increase in your compensation for the additional work.
- You'll get some support in staying at the same level of responsibility but with a different configuration of tasks.
- You'll get valuable insight into how your boss prioritizes your tasks when they help you re-sort and reorder yours.

●— **PUTTING IT INTO PRACTICE: SAYING NO**

Practice saying no to the following types of people, and write down or record how you'll say it:

- Boss
- Coworker
- Partner/Spouse
- Parent
- Child
- Other family member
- Friend
- Frenemy
- Neighbor

If role-playing doesn't feel too hokey or contrived, give it a try. There is tremendous power and competence gained by saying the words out loud rather than just thinking them. It will be much easier to say them to someone else when you've already heard yourself saying them out loud.

Use either an actual or a familiar request you've gotten from these people to get you started.

THE BOTTOM LINE

The only thing better than good news is bad news fast.

You aren't helping anyone by saying "maybe" when the answer will ultimately be "no."

We all know how it feels when someone does it to us—we think they're rearranging their schedule to accommodate our request and they're really just burning through a few days, thinking the lapsed time will soften the blow when they tell us no. It's a waste of everyone's time and just slows us down on the search for a "yes."

Practice saying no right away to things you don't want to do or don't have time for.

Practice stopping yourself before you say "because" or give an excuse or explanation for why the answer is no. You don't have to be smug or mean—you also don't need to be a doormat.

Never lie to yourself, thinking that you don't control your own life and, by extension, your schedule. With very few exceptions (on-call emergency doctors, for instance), you do. There may be consequences to saying no, but there are also consequences to saying yes. Decide for yourself which is better or worse and *then* make your choice.

CHAPTER RECAP

If you are enthusiastic and easily excited, and also avoid conflict in your relationships at all costs, you are especially vulnerable to over-committing.

It's fun to volunteer and it's nice to feel needed. There's an inherent ego boost in having others rely on us or being the go-to resource for help or guidance.

But when you take on more and more tasks without carefully considering all the implications of your choices, you can easily create the very sense of overwhelm you probably picked up this book to address.

When it comes to your commitments, remember: you have chosen everything that you said yes and no to. Even if it doesn't *feel* like you have a choice, as with caring for an ailing family member or handling the extra work your boss throws at you, you still have the agency to choose. You *can* say no. So practice saying no and leaving empty spaces in your calendar.

You might not like the consequences of saying no, but that is what you're actually choosing between—the consequences of saying yes and the consequences of saying no. The task itself may have less impact than what saying yes to it does to your schedule, confidence, self-esteem, motivation, and, most importantly, your stress level.

When you do say yes, own that decision. Owning your choices keeps you in control, even when making the best of a crappy situation. This simple adjustment will have a huge long-term impact on your mental health.

Also, remember that saying yes and being needed delivers a dopamine hit that our brains come to rely on. When we chase that rush too often, we can find ourselves out of control of our own time, rushing around, juggling everyone else's priorities ahead of our own, and racing head-long into burnout. The rewards don't last and the consequences make us suffer. One thing's for sure: if your calendar is packed full, you're taking on too much.

Among the results of overcommitting are the following:

- Constantly running behind
- Showing up unprepared
- Decreased ability to manage stress
- Feeling overloaded and mentally absent
- Relationship friction and repeatedly disappointing others
- Compromised and lesser-quality work

If you're a chronic overcommitter, you've almost certainly had to sacrifice quality in order to complete all of your commitments. When there is too much to do and not enough time to do it all, something has to give. Being overextended feels unbalanced—because it is.

The longer you stay in that wobbly position, the longer you put stress on your body and your mind. And when you are consistently or even constantly stretched beyond your capacity, you will crash hard into your unrealistic expectations. When that happens, you are more likely to feel disappointment and shame than satisfaction at having completed the assignment. If this is already a pattern in your life, it needs to be dismantled as quickly as possible.

Worse yet, you aren't really showing up for others when you're over-reaching because, often, you're not actually present enough to do so. While you may be there physically, your attention is fractured and just as likely to be focused on where you just came from or where you're heading to next. When you aren't completely present, you're creating the ideal conditions for things to fall through the cracks. All in the service of maintaining a relentless and demanding schedule you created for yourself.

It shouldn't be a surprise that, regardless of how strong you are, that kind of pace will eventually lead to burnout. And from there, you're even more useless to everyone, including yourself.

HOW TO STOP OVERCOMMITTING

- Take control of your calendar. Drive your day from it and guard against anything getting in it that you are not 100 percent committed to.
- Refine your ability to prioritize. Make sure you're spending time doing things that are important, and that you're not filling your time up with insignificant tasks. Any new task has to earn its right to be done by you and must be equal to or greater in importance than what you're already committed to.
- Start saying no—and mean it. You may have to practice this to feel okay saying it, but it is much better to deal with the discomfort of saying no now than the pain you'll feel by adding too many things to your calendar . . . again. One pain subsides quickly, the other has lasting consequences and is around until you finish the task.
- Wait 24 hours before saying yes. It's okay to express curiosity or enthusiasm, but give yourself at least a day to review your existing commitments and how any new opportunities could be integrated into your calendar.
- Leverage your values when deciding what to take on. There will always be more to do than there are hours in the day. And while many things may be important, if the task doesn't align with your values, you can say no and trust that the person asking will find the right person to help. You do not need to rescue every person and every organization from a current or ongoing crisis that you did not cause.
- Learn to delegate. Continuing with the previous point, you could choose to underwrite the expense of hiring someone to complete the task you neither want to do nor have the time for. Either way, you can usually find someone else, paid

or unpaid, to pass a task along to. Saying that you must do it or it won't get done is almost certainly one of your 200 lies.

- Don't overpack your calendar. Leave some unstructured time in your calendar for either rest or the unexpected. If there's no room to breathe, you're likely to choke on all your obligations—and that won't be fun or useful.
- Treat "no" as a complete sentence. Not only can you say no as discussed above—you can say no and not offer an excuse or explanation. You can simply say, "Thank you, and I'm going to gratefully decline."

Overcommitting is closely linked to poor planning (our next time thief), because without a plan and a way to track your progress, it's easy to overbook yourself and take on too much.

Chapter 7
Poor Planning

"It is better to look ahead and prepare
than to look back and regret."
Jackie Joyner-Kersee

Interruptions are the most prevalent time thief, but poor planning creates the biggest and worst problems consistently.

Learning how to plan successfully is the key to managing your time.

There's poor planning and then there's no planning. It's hard to tell which one delivers worse results.

If the idea of planning your days ahead of time makes you cringe or feels like a noose around your neck, I'll bet you've got a story running that says planning is the death of spontaneity—but that's incorrect.

According to Swiss philosopher Henri-Frédéric Amiel, over-analysis is what kills spontaneity.[36]

Planning also doesn't mean living like a robot or micromanaging your every movement and decision.

Nor does planning necessarily equal rigid routines, such as the following:

- Eating the same meals at the same times each day

- Laying out your clothes every night before bed
- Reducing your wardrobe down to a "uniform" of the same top, bottom, and underwear
- Doing household chores and errands on a set schedule and never varying it

If you find comfort in any of these kinds of routines, that's great—they're just not required to plan your day . . . or your life.

Now that we know what planning isn't, let's home in on what planning is.

The *Oxford English Dictionary* defines planning as "the process of making plans for something."

Never helpful when they use the noun source of the verb in the definition, so let's dig a bit deeper.

This is how Merriam-Webster defines "plan":

    a. a method for achieving an end
    b. an often customary method of doing something
    c. a detailed formulation of a program of action
    d. an orderly arrangement of parts of an overall design or objective

Better. For our purposes, let's say that planning is "the process of pulling together an orderly arrangement of steps and parts needed to achieve a clearly defined end."

We could also say it's figuring out what you're going to do on any given day and at what time and in what order.

So whether you are planning a birthday party or your retirement, it's important to account for all the steps you have to take to go from idea to execution to completion.

Planning gives you control over your life—and is the antidote to either "flying by the seat of your pants" or the "shoot first, ask questions later" approach to life.

Planning also gives you control of your time. When you have planned something out, you are spending or investing that time exactly as you wish.

It puts you in the driver's seat with your hands on the wheel. If you're not driving, you're relying on luck, chance, hope, and fear to steer you in the right direction.

Of course, some folks pray as an alternative to planning, and then when things work out, they attribute their success to some god's intervention, and when it doesn't, they claim that either it wasn't that god's will or they hadn't prayed hard enough.

Waiting, hoping, or praying for divine intervention is not a substitute for your own agency. Don't they say, "God helps those who help themselves"?

I'm going to remain agnostic about any alternative methods to actual planning.

And again, for the free spirits, just don't overanalyze and you won't lose the ability to be spontaneous.

So now we know at least two things:

- There is a big difference between planning and boxing yourself into a regimented, rigid life.
- Planning enables spontaneity, rather than killing it.

When you plan, you are free to grab any opportunities that come your way. You are already in the habit of actively choosing what you're focusing on and when.

So when something exciting presents itself and is aligned with your values and goals, it's relatively easy to say yes.

You may have to do a little rearranging in your calendar, but that's just mechanical.

Since the biggest obstacle to change is often our feelings, if this new opportunity sounds good, jumping any necessary hurdles should be easy, at least emotionally.

Planning reduces feelings of guilt and anxiety because when you're following the plan, you're "right where you should be."

And if "planning equals boring" is still bouncing around inside your brain, you may be more of a drama queen than a free spirit. Just saying.

WHAT PLANNING ALLOWS

If what you focus on is what you manifest, without a plan you're focusing on nothing or what's already in front of you. Neither seems like the best way to make something new happen quickly and efficiently, does it?

Serendipity and planning aren't mutually exclusive. Magic can happen *inside* a plan; it just doesn't *replace* the plan.

Art and planning are not opposite poles on a spectrum, either.

Picasso was the first artist to become a millionaire while he was alive. You can have opinions about his other life choices, but there is no denying that he was exceptionally talented and prolific.

He also did something few other artists have ever done—created a new form of art, Cubism.

He did this methodically, by planning and by using math and his superior draftsmanship in the service of his creativity.

While his desire to see and represent things differently was inspired, inspiration isn't how Cubism came to be. Cubism happened through trial and error and planning.

And Cubism as conceived by Picasso was possible because he could draw something accurately first.

You can't cube something effectively if you can't see or represent it clearly in two dimensions to begin with.

This is just one example of how planning, talent, and creativity yield repeatable, predictable, and excellent results.

Whether or not you consider yourself an artist, if you think your work or your life might benefit from streamlining certain recurring tasks and projects, you'll do that by planning and by creating SOPs (standard operating procedures).

If you want to explore possible outcomes before committing to something, planning and testing are how you can do that.

Planning will cure chronic lateness, double booking, FOMO, and all those annoying forms of worrying and what-ifs.

And if the only thing standing between you and embracing planning as a useful time management tool is a story about what you might lose—which is mostly in your imagination anyway—focus on everything you will gain, which is a surprising amount of time and freedom.

Freedom to choose exactly what you will do, when, and how.

10 OUTCOMES OF POOR PLANNING

Here are 10 of the worst outcomes of poor planning, along with the benefits you'll instantly get when you stop this behavior.

OUTCOME: Without a plan, you rely on luck or magic for results—neither of which is predictable.

VERSUS: Getting predictable results every time.

This seems like the biggest form of unregulated gambling—and while I believe in intuition and trusting your gut, those are both more helpful guides for *what* to do than *how* to do it.

Back to the car as a metaphor. Imagine being in the car with your hands in your lap—and now you're barreling down the road hoping it doesn't crash while also taking the shortest, most direct route to where you want to be.

That sounds potentially dangerous, right?

Would you want to be on a road with cars and drivers moving fast but no one actually driving? I wouldn't, either.

OUTCOME: Without a plan, you're at the mercy of outside influences—for better and worse.

VERSUS: Saving time, money, and energy by avoiding predictable surprises.

Think back to the last time you didn't plan something and a "surprise" happened, particularly a surprise that brought unwanted complications. How much time or money, not to mention effort, did you spend trying to fix or undo those complications? All of those resources could have been saved with a bit of planning.

Now, you can't plan *everything* in your life or prevent the unexpected from ever occurring. But with a plan, especially one that includes a plan B, you'll be much better prepared for any curve balls life throws at you.

I moved out of my apartment in NYC in November 2019. I let go of a lot of furniture and other items, then stored the rest. I was planning to travel for all of 2020, teaching, speaking, and writing.

I headed off to Florida as my first stop, curious to try being a "snowbird" for the first time—with plans to head west on March 15, 2020.

After a few months of renting a place in St. Petersburg, I liked it enough that I decided to buy a place of my own. I figured I could do what my current landlord was doing—use it between gigs, and then rent it out when I was on the road.

And then COVID hit. Suddenly there was nowhere to go—no speaking or teaching gigs and no prospects either.

So instead leaving town, I went back to New York and got my stuff out of storage, then settled into my new place for the pandemic.

Three things happened as a result:

- I spent less money on the move and my mortgage than I would have spent storing things in New York and renting someone else's place for the year.
- I got to furnish my new place with my own belongings, so at least something was familiar when everything else was up in the air.
- I was now set up so I could rent the place when I was able to start traveling again for work.

No one could have predicted what happened with COVID—the tragic loss of life and livelihoods around the globe. I was one of the lucky ones. And because I had a plan, even though it was turned on its head, I was able to pivot quickly and avoid some of the worst consequences of being somewhere unexpected during lockdown.

I had exactly one friend in St. Pete—and no way to meet anyone new, since every public place was closed.

So while I felt a bit stranded emotionally and physically, at least I had a roof over my head and a way of working remotely. That kept me afloat in a new town until restrictions relaxed enough that I could venture out and make some new friends.

OUTCOME: You might get everything done but not as quickly or efficiently.

VERSUS: Saving time and energy . . . again.

When you don't plan out the right order of events in advance, you'll waste time in the moment trying to figure out what to do next.

If you struggle with indecision, it may be harder to decide the best course of action when you're feeling under the gun or on the spot—and even more so if others are waiting on your decision, too.

You may have to repeat or redo certain tasks because you did them out of order.

You may not remember how you did something the last time, so you'll waste time trying to recreate your exact method for doing it again now.

You may even do things you don't need to do at all—but you won't discover that until you've already done it and spent the resources figuring that out. Those resources could have been conserved with advance planning.

OUTCOME: You'll misallocate your time.

VERSUS: Saving more time and energy.

As a professional organizer and productivity coach, I constantly hear people complain that they don't have enough time to do the things they want to do.

But when we sit down and look at their calendars together, we can see that they absolutely do have the time—they're just often wasting it by doing the wrong tasks in the wrong order at the wrong times. Or they're doing things that don't need to be done, out of either confusion or boredom.

As it's been said before, you can't do everything, but you should be able to do everything important—with planning.

OUTCOME: You'll pay more than you need to or you'll spend money prematurely.

VERSUS: Saving more money.

My friend and client Wilma wanted to renovate her kitchen. We talked through all the changes she wanted to make and came up with a plan, including when to purchase new appliances—which wouldn't happen until we had finalized the floor plan and the cabinets had been ordered. Can you guess what happened next?

She didn't follow the plan and bought about $25,000 worth of high-end appliances because "they were on sale," as if this was the last time appliances would ever go on sale. The truth is, she wanted the rush from spending the money and showing off to her partner. For a few minutes, Wilma got to be a big shot when she displayed her new purchases.

She got that hit of dopamine . . . and then ended up spending all of the money she saved and more when she had to store those appliances for $400 a month with no renovation in sight. Wait, it gets better.

She then broke up with her partner and decided to sell her house.

So now she is paying $400 a month *and* has to sell those appliances at a loss just to get rid of them. She can't even install them in her current kitchen as an upgrade because they are too big for the existing openings. Ouch.

OUTCOME: You'll be at the mercy of other people's schedules and demands.

VERSUS: Retaining control over your time and resources.

If only everyone knew the difference between a request and a demand, right?

Email (which we'll dig into in the next chapter) is a great example of this. Without a plan, you could easily spend an entire eight-hour day in your inbox, and never get any other tasks done.

Not to mention that email begets email—almost every time you send one out or reply to one, you will soon have another email to deal with.

When you plan how and when you'll use a tool, you are in control.

When you don't, you'll have two factors to deal with: the time demands required to use the tool itself and the expectations that other people create to fill the vacuum left by the absence of *your* plan.

OUTCOME: You'll second-guess yourself, feel anxious, and lack confidence while tasking.

VERSUS: Having less anxiety, more confidence, and more competence, too.

The first time you do anything, it's unlikely you'll feel completely at ease and capable—remember beginner's mind?

Those feelings of being unsure or hesitant can be amplified when something big is riding on your decisions and actions.

It's no big deal if you don't know the rules of a new card game you're learning.

If you're pulling together a report that your company will use for financial modeling and revenue projections, and you're doing it without a clear plan, you might be appropriately skeptical of your process and your results.

Planning the steps you'll take in advance of doing the task and having a system for checking your work as you go along are two ways to avoid obvious mistakes and the kinds of errors that happen when you're rushing or not paying full attention to what you're doing.

You may not feel completely confident in your abilities to do the task well, but you should at least feel confident that you know what needs to be done and in what order.

This lets you distinguish the nervousness that comes with trying something new from the nervousness of trying something new and not knowing how to do it, either.

OUTCOME: You double-book, overextend yourself, and struggle to feel grounded when traveling or straddling multiple time zones.

VERSUS: Feeling in control of your schedule and commitments regardless of where you are physically.

If you work remotely or internationally, chances are you're going to have meetings, as well as tasks and deadlines, in various time zones. If you're not organized, aware of and realistic about your limitations, and driving your day from your calendar, scheduling and producing work can become complicated. You may even disrupt your sleep patterns and risk burning out.

Simply put, we tend to overestimate our ability to adapt and underestimate the impact that any change of schedule or location creates.

When I was writing this book, I was 13 to 16 hours away from my team. Before I left the US, I optimistically scheduled recurring calls at a time that would be convenient for one of my colleagues back home, even though it would then be late in the evening for me.

When that first appointment rolled around, I had been writing all day and was too tired to discuss or do anything complex. So we ended up using that first meeting to reschedule all of the remaining calls to a time that was only a little inconvenient for us both.

The more you can plan and anticipate your energy level and ability to concentrate, given all the other variables resulting from being away from your routines, the more you can avoid or mitigate wasted time or other negative effects when working across time zones.

OUTCOME: Your morale and your relationships will suffer.

VERSUS: Experiencing more harmony, less friction and less stress with yourself and others.

Regardless of how creative, free-spirited, and charming you think you are, the cumulative effect of being consistently inconsistent will wear everyone down over time.

Other people who either love you or have to interact with you will develop coping strategies to minimize your unpredictable influence on their lives.

You may become the person they lie to, saying that the meeting is at 5:30 p.m. when it's really at 6:00 p.m.—so your lack of planning doesn't derail everything else.

You may also get fewer invitations.

Eye rolling and sarcasm are passive-aggressive forms of communication, and you may get some of both when people talk about you and your lack of planning.

Just like that episode of *Friends* where Phoebe tried to turn around the definition of "pulling a Monica," your way of showing up may become a running joke among your tribe, with people saying, "Oh, well, that's a total *fill in your name here* . . . You know how they are."

We derive self-esteem from doing esteemable acts. Your image of yourself may take a beating as faith in your own abilities and reliability declines.

OUTCOME: You will miss a key step in a process that then requires a do-over.

VERSUS: Getting things done the right way the first time, plus all the above benefits.

I'm not sure when it would be time well spent to retrace your steps to find something missed or overlooked when planning out those steps in advance could have prevented the mistake in the first place.

It's always cheaper and more fun to use your imagination up front to predict possible omissions and errors. Depending on the nature of your life and your work, the scale of those costs and savings could be huge.

OUTCOME: You'll develop avoidable regrets and limit your personal growth.

VERSUS: Achieving self-actualization and freedom from needless regret.

Whether you're dreaming of a lush garden or curating, as Mary Oliver says, "your one wild and precious life," how can you ensure you'll achieve your goals without planning?[37]

This doesn't mean you'll follow your plan to the letter or that there won't be unexpected developments along the way.

But through planning, your days will have focus and meaning—there will be a sense of deliberateness and intention to your actions. Less treading water and more swimming toward a specific point.

You'll be free to say yes to things based on your values that could open the door to your wildest dreams, and say no to distractions masquerading as opportunities that lead nowhere.

You'll see that you have much to be grateful for every day and you'll easily recognize the lie that "nothing is ever easy for me," since some things *are* easy for you . . . when you take the time to plan them out.

Besides, easy is relative. It certainly wasn't easy or fast baking a cake over a lightbulb in my friend Lisa's Easy-Bake Oven.

Hopefully it's clear by now that planning isn't just a good idea—it's an essential ingredient in a rich, purposeful, and engaged life.

WHY PLANNING MATTERS

We all get the exact same number of hours in a week: 168. How well we use them is up to us.

Part of that equation depends on your willingness and ability to plan.

It's seldom a good idea to compare yourself with others—you'll never really know what's going on in someone else's life, and keeping score often looks like building an argument for why you suck and someone else doesn't.

Other people might accomplish more than you do in your 168 hours . . . this week.

The only thing we know for sure is that it's not because they have more time. It could be because you have greater demands on your time or because they are using those hours more strategically.

Want to know the secret behind their strategy? Planning.

Let's say you're working a demanding full-time job, or even two of them. Together they total 100 hours a week between work and commuting. You still have 68 hours that are all yours. Of course, you need to rest and take care of your other responsibilities, but those 68 hours are yours to do with as you think best.

Sylvia Pettigrew is a perfect example of this. Sylvia works two full-time jobs and is a single mother. She was also committed to getting and staying organized. She enrolled in the Unstuff Your Life System and, after some planning, figured out that she had seven minutes a day between jobs that she could dedicate to decluttering and organizing.[38]

Instead of lamenting that meager number, she dug in. Consistently.

Over the 10-week program, she completely reclaimed her basement. It went from being a neglected dumping ground for random junk to a clean, tidy live/work space where she and her son now relax, watch movies, hang out, and play.

In seven minutes a day.

As a result of Sylvia's progress, her aunt asked her to visit St. Louis and work her magic there. You can see her before-and-after pics at cbobbook.com/planning.

Now, if your first reaction to this is, "Well, that's great for her, but that could never work for me because . . . ," that just means you may have some mindset work to do.

Sylvia will be the first to tell you that she didn't think she could do it, either.

She looked at other people in the program and would compare her circumstances with theirs—at least what she could see of them—and she always came up short.

Over the 10 weeks, we worked on her mindset and focused on what she *did* have control over—those seven minutes.

And the results speak for themselves.

So it's okay if you are skeptical. Do the planning anyway.

If you do what you usually do, you'll get what you usually get. If you don't want that, you have nothing to lose and everything to gain by acting "as if."

As if you could get what you want through planning. Chances are you have more time than you think you do.

In almost three decades of doing this work, I've only seen one person who had less time than they thought, and that was my client Judy in Laguna Beach.

Judy is a wife and a mom with two kids who have multiple congenital disabilities—one child can't walk without assistance and, tragically, neither child will likely live to adulthood.

Her husband has an exceptional job, so money isn't an issue for them, which makes it easier to afford the around-the-clock care the children require. One child's immune system is so compromised that all her food is prepared in isolation to avoid cross-contamination and is carefully measured down to the gram.

When we first met, Judy was understandably overwhelmed and completely stressed out. She was doing her best to run the household and care for her kids without a plan, but that meant that every day felt like they were starting from scratch.

We sat down and mapped out everything that was needed to keep her children alive and the household functioning.

As we did the math, we figured out that after all of her responsibilities for her children, her husband, and the house were accounted for, she had one hour in the day that belonged to her alone.

Prior to doing this work, she felt stupid, inadequate, and like a failure. She had a story running that she was horrible at time management. Because how could she not have a "traditional paid" job and still be exhausted each night? Where was all that time going?

And because money wasn't an issue, she felt even worse—as if she were actively squandering her resources.

Relief washed over her and her stress dissolved when she discovered that she wasn't crazy or inefficient—there were literally only 60 minutes in every 24 hours that weren't already committed to a competing demand.

We created a short list of things she could do for herself to recharge during that one hour each day, which included a solo walk around the block, a short yoga class online or down the hill, some meditation, or even a quick nap.

If you have more free time than Judy, count yourself lucky. And let's do everything we can so you maximize those hours and they don't just slip away unconsciously.

Like most things, it's not always obvious where the time goes. Big chunks of time are often easier to track down than the 5- and 10-minute "little" blips that are actually robbing you senseless.

By themselves, they seem inconsequential. But you're nickel-and-diming yourself out of a year of your life in 5- and 10-minute bits—that's what they add up to for the average person.

This is one place where you don't want to be average.

You also can't manage what you don't measure. The Pareto Principle suggests that 80 percent of your desired results come from the most impactful 20 percent of your efforts.

This has been adopted by many sales teams to direct their prospecting and nurturing efforts.

By leveraging the Pareto Principle, some sales teams focus on their most loyal and reliable customers who also consistently spend the most, figuring that they are responsible for up to 80 percent of their gross sales.

If that's true, figuring out your most impactful 20 percent and focusing on it may move the needle more for you than just being busy all the time.

My 20 percent for our business involves just two things—speaking at events like conferences and trade shows, and actively networking.

When people see me speaking or meet me and learn what I do, it typically leads to an engagement. Contrast that with blog writing, social media posting, and even appearing on mainstream media channels—all things I do but that don't produce nearly the same revenue (or in some cases, *any* direct revenue) for a similar investment of time.

If all hours are equal, it isn't hard to figure out that outsourcing blog writing and social media posting would free me up to get on even more stages, virtually or in person, and that that would deliver the greatest ROI on my time spent for the company.

In the next section, we'll look at how *you* can figure out where you get the greatest return on your time spent.

ELEPHANTS REMEMBER, BUT YOU PROBABLY WON'T

Here is a bit of brain science that proves you're not going to remember things if you don't write them down.[39] You'll remember moments tied to big feelings—though probably not very reliably.

Our brains haven't evolved to hold large volumes of data indefinitely. They're designed to make quick fight-or-flight decisions and then act.

So if you ever say to yourself, "I'll remember that when I need it," and then struggle to recall what it was that you thought was so important, the solution is to write it down. But only in one place, ever.

If you are someone who often writes the same list over and over or has multiple notebooks going, with much of the same information in each of them because you can't find the right list when you're looking for it, that's become an inefficient workaround for our brain's design.

You may "remember" that you already made the list but if you're not using the Organizational Triangle to keep track of your list, you won't be able to find it in 30 seconds or less.

And while I support your desire to capture something important, writing it down over and over in this way is not solving the problem—it's just wasting time and creating clutter.

The better choice is to write it down once, put it with its siblings where you can easily find it, and then let it go until you need it again.

HOW TO START PLANNING EFFECTIVELY

If you want to know how long it takes to do something, time it. Use a stopwatch (or stopwatch function on a digital timer) and record how long you spend doing a task.

This is less important for tasks you'll only do once—although if you do similar tasks, like building websites, there is value in tracking these kinds of activities, too.

For recurring tasks, it's important to figure out how long something takes to do.

Knowing that it takes you, on average, 49 minutes to do a load of laundry is more useful than guesstimating that it takes you "about an hour" to do it.

When you start with the math, it becomes easier to budget enough time to get things done without overestimating and ending up with *time to kill*. None of us have enough time to murder it.

Time yourself for one week and see how much information you can gather. We talked about this in Chapter 2. Think of it as a noble experiment rather than a challenge and you'll be less likely to resist the exercise or judge yourself for what you discover.

This is not a *gotcha* exercise, and you're not trying to find out how wrong you've been at guessing over the years.

The past is past—glance back, but don't dwell and don't go digging through past mistakes for opportunities to shame or humiliate yourself. When you know better, you do better, so forgive yourself for what you did or didn't do when you knew less.

And while planning may sound big and complicated, there are really just a few things you need to do to plan efficiently and effectively.

Start by learning the best way to use to-do lists and calendars.

TO-DO LISTS

To-do lists are to your tasks what your closets are to your clothes—they're the homes for these items before you use them.

You still have to go into the closet to pick out an outfit, and you still have to go to your lists and select tasks to schedule and complete.

Since you don't wear every piece of clothing you own each day, you shouldn't be dragging around your to-do lists, either. Whatever you've pulled from a list to do should be scheduled on your calendar so you can leave the lists at home.

And given that you probably already have one or more to-do lists lying around, we'll start with those and then discuss any new lists you make going forward.

Either way, to-do lists are a bit of a misnomer, because these lists aren't really about doing—that's what your calendar is for.

For any existing lists, you'll want to review them and then pull each task off the list and drop it into a "time bucket"—which is just a single category container. That way, all similar tasks are grouped together so you can then prioritize them, like with like.

Going forward, when a new task or errand comes up, put it directly into its corresponding time bucket and prioritize it immediately in relation to all the other tasks already in that time bucket.

There may be times when you need to create a new list and that's okay. Just dump everything out of your head onto a piece of paper or a digital file. Don't worry about sorting or arranging each task or errand into like-with-like categories while you're writing, unless it's easy or natural for you to do so. The primary goal is to get everything off your mind so you aren't struggling to remember it all. Keep writing until you can't think of anything else you have to do or remember and, only then, sort.

As you did with any previous lists, start by pulling individual tasks off the list and dropping them into their matching time buckets. You may discover that some of the things on your new list are already in a time bucket. Sometimes we subconsciously second-guess or don't trust ourselves and continue holding on to tasks that are important because we're worried we'll otherwise forget them. When that happens, don't stress about it. Just cross it off your list and keep moving.

Once the list is empty and you've confirmed that everything on it has been accounted for in a time bucket, throw the empty list or piece of paper away. Don't save it "just in case"—it becomes clutter at that point.

Then go into each time bucket and reprioritize any new tasks in relation to the tasks already in the bucket.

This way, you use the same principles for managing time as you use to get and stay organized. Just like with clutter, it is much easier to figure out what is more or less important when comparing similar items.

It can be difficult to decide if an individual sweater should stay or go when it's by itself.

But once you group your sweaters together and see all your black turtlenecks side by side, not all in the same condition and not equally flattering, it is easier to let some go in favor of keeping others.

The same principle applies to your to-dos. It's much easier to prioritize tasks when they are grouped together into categories and isolated from unrelated tasks.

TIME BUCKETS

Time buckets are discrete 3-D corrals for categories of similar tasks. Here are two starter sets of time buckets—one for work and one for your personal life. Feel free to add or subtract based on your individual needs.

Don't feel like you need to use all of these buckets. Just be thorough and comprehensive in identifying the kinds of tasks and activities you're engaged in regularly.

These lists are in alphabetical order, not in any order of priority—you can do that once you've created your own set of buckets.

WORK

Admin & Clerical, WORK, including Sorting & Filing
Advertising
Business Development
Client Services
Errands
Financial
Marketing
Planning
Professional Development
Project 1
Project 2
Public Relations
Research
Volunteering & Community
Other

LIFE

Admin & Clerical, LIFE, including Sorting & Filing
Creative Expression
Errands
Education
Financial
Friends & Family
Giving Back
Health & Fitness
Home Maintenance
Medical
Organizing & Simplifying
Project 1
Project 2
Self-Care
Self-Development
Spiritual Practices
Volunteering & Community
Other

Once you've got your list of buckets, you're ready to start.

WORKING WITH TIME BUCKETS AND TO-DO LISTS

These steps were laid out in narrative form above. They are repeated here in list form. Follow these steps and you'll be amazed at how quickly this goes and how easy it is to categorize and prioritize your tasks once they are grouped with their siblings:

1. Create your list of time buckets.
2. Gather all your to-do lists—you may have only one or, like many people, you may have multiple lists floating around.
3. If you do have multiple lists and they are already category- or time bucket–specific, move the contents of an entire list right into its corresponding bucket.
4. If you have multiple lists and they are not category-specific, review and harvest items one by one from these lists, crossing out any duplicate tasks as you come across them. When a list is empty, toss it in the recycle bin or delete it.
5. Once all your current to-dos are in their appropriate buckets, assign durations to as many as you can based on your noble experiment of timing your tasks.
6. When you've quantified as many tasks as you can, start to prioritize the tasks in their buckets.
7. When all the tasks are prioritized inside their buckets, you can prioritize the buckets themselves.
8. Use your values and any external deadlines to determine priority in Steps 6 and 7.

●— PUTTING IT INTO PRACTICE: CLEANING UP YOUR BUCKETS

We started this book by talking about values, and you'll want to return to those now. Start by setting your timer for 15 minutes. Then answer these questions and review your time buckets using your answers as a filter or lens to evaluate both the buckets and the contents of each bucket.

- What matters most to you?
- How do these buckets and tasks line up with what matters to you?
- Do you have buckets and tasks that are stuffed and overflowing?
- Do you have buckets and tasks that have nothing to do with your values?
- Do you have buckets that are under-utilized for categories that matter a lot to you?

If you answered yes to any of the last three questions, what can you do to resolve that situation?

For individual tasks that have little to do with your current values, how quickly can you do them if you must, delegate them away, or delete them?

WORKING WITH YOUR CALENDAR

It's great to have all your to-dos in one place.

It's great to have all your to-dos divided up into their proper time buckets.

It's great to have those to-dos quantified and prioritized according to your values and any external deadlines.

Now it's time to use your calendar and plan.

Your calendar becomes the visual representation of your plan and your roadmap for your day, week, month, and year. It will reflect all the research, thinking, and deciding you've done prior to scheduling and then doing a task.

SETTING UP AND USING YOUR CALENDAR

Start by blocking out time for recurring high-value activities or golf balls. If you don't know which tasks you'll slot into each block of time yet, that's okay. The most important thing is to allocate enough time for these categories that you can fit other time bucket contents around them.

The largest blocks of time will likely be work, family, life admin, spiritual practices, self-care, health & fitness, and sleep. Don't worry if your buckets don't match my examples. Your calendar should reflect your values and buckets—your golf balls—not mine or anyone else's.

Pay attention while scheduling to anywhere that you can potentially save time. What have you already timed? What has been optimized—tracked and studied—and where do you either know or sense you often waste time, get snagged, or run into bottlenecks?

Each bump in the road is an opportunity to look for ways to shave off some time by making minor adjustments and hacking your day.

Here's an example of how you can do this exercise to recapture lost time.

Chris, a principal at an insurance agency, was responsible for driving the family to church every Sunday morning. The service starts at 10 a.m.—no surprises or variation there.

His wife did grocery shopping later in the day on Sunday, once everyone was home and settled into whatever else they were going to do after church.

While not that far, the drive to church was 15 miles and approximately 22 minutes door to door. On the way, they would pass Costco, a membership bulk store, and Publix, their regular grocery store.

When we were working together, and Chris was complaining that the family only had a few hours together on Saturday and again on Sunday, we drilled down into what those days looked like.

I asked him this question: instead of returning home from church and then his wife heading back out, what if they did their shopping for the week on the way home? That way they could accomplish three things at one time:

- They'd all spend more time together. Whether they all went into the stores together or his wife ran in and he played ball with the kids in the parking lot or helped them with school projects, they'd feel like they were all involved in the chores in a different way and that feeling of closeness after church could continue even while tasking.
- His wife would have some help if anything large needed carrying, and she'd also get a little alone time while Chris and the kids were outside. She'd feel the family's presence while doing something for all of them but wouldn't have them underfoot as she made her way through the stores efficiently.
- They'd save money and time on the double commute, since they were working their way back home anyway.

And here's the net savings:

19 minutes to Costco/Publix each way   **= 38 minutes round trip**
14 miles to Costco/Publix each way   **= 28 miles round trip**
1.25 gallons of gasoline   **= $5.00**

Would it be useful for you to save 38 minutes, drive 28 fewer miles, and save $5.00 a week, just by changing one routine on one day?

How about spending more time together engaged in living the family's values? Those were both important to Chris and his family, and in some ways worth a lot more than the literal savings.

Over one year, the savings add up to 30.4 hours and $240, just from hacking one task. If you have 10 recurring tasks a week, how much more time and money can you put back into your pocket by examining them this way?

Once you've added all the recurring appointments to your calendar, it's time to visit your time buckets and start fishing out any other priority level–1 and -2 one-off golf-ball tasks you want to get done today and this week.

For an example of how this looks on my calendar, visit cbobbook. com/planning.

After you get the hang of scheduling this way, you can use this system to plan further out.

For now, let's do a day or a week at a time so you can walk before running.

After all this scheduling has been done, if you still have some time slots available on your calendar and you want to fit more in, go back to your time buckets for any level-3 to-dos.

Anything that is a 4 or 5 in your buckets should be delegated or removed completely—you will never get to them, nor should you. They may have been around for a while, but that doesn't make them important, just persistent. Give them away or eliminate them.

STOPPING NEGATIVE SELF-TALK BEFORE IT DERAILS YOUR EFFORTS

Pay attention to any shame or guilt that comes up while doing this work. Taking control of your calendar and, by extension, your life can stir up some feelings.

I promise you, though, that any trash talk you're hearing in your head is someone else's voice. You have a divine or human right to be happy and to live your life as you choose.

So if there's any aggressive garbage coming at you saying, "Who do you think you are?" or "How dare you?" as you create boundaries and let go of tasks that don't serve you, that is definitely not your original, natural voice—that was planted by some other person.

Those voices can undermine your best planning and destroy your self-esteem when they're allowed to continue talking unchecked.

TRASH TALK IN THE POCONOS

My own experiences with those voices could be seen during the time I owned a house in Pike County, PA.

In 2002, I bought a house in Dingmans Ferry after a relationship blew up and I decided not to relocate to Seattle. During the eight years I owned that house, I was involved in two lawsuits and the house underwent a gut renovation. Oh, and I wrote *Unstuff Your Life!* there.

The first lawsuit was with the people I bought the house from. They had hidden a broken and unstable foundation, which I luckily discovered within the first three months of ownership. Once we settled the first lawsuit, my plan was to use the settlement money to renovate the house.

Of course, the settlement wasn't nearly enough to cover the costs of jacking up the house, blowing out the existing foundation, laying a new foundation, and then setting the house back down on the now stable base. Both while pursuing the sellers and then managing the renovation, I would talk with a few trusted friends about how challenging it was to maintain a positive outlook and believe that everything would eventually work out.

There were more than a few nights when I had to talk myself off the metaphorical ledge and breathe my way into radical acceptance, tapping every ounce of patience I could find.

The second suit was against the sons of the developer of our planned community. These two men had neglected our collective amenities—tennis courts, swimming pool, roads, and three lakes—until they were almost unusable.

After several years, that suit was also settled. The community formed a property owner's association and I was elected its first president. There were still neighbors in the development who were loyal to the brothers, and our monthly board meetings were often contentious and verging on violent.

My inner dialogue at the time would flip between absolute certainty that we were doing the right thing and deep self-doubt, thinking that every choice I was making would lead to me losing all of my money and becoming homeless.

I navigated a lot of emotional and physical crap during those eight years in rural PA. I also made some amazing friends and invested a lot of time and money turning that house into a beautiful and structurally sound home for myself.

So it was a big surprise to me one Sunday morning, while standing in my shower in Manhattan, that I found myself arguing with the then treasurer of the board about something so trivial I can't even remember now what it was about.

Of course, he wasn't in the shower with me—this entire disagreement was taking place between my ears, in my imagination.

And that's when I had the thought—I could resign from the board.

After all, I had done everything I committed to doing: getting our amenities under control, establishing a board, writing by-laws, and establishing systems so we could effectively and efficiently self-govern.

What surprised me even more was my next thought—I could sell my house.

That was shocking. And once I really considered it, liberating.

It didn't mean that I didn't love that house—I did. I literally rebuilt it from the ground up, made every design choice, and served as the general contractor for the renovation (with some strategic help from a friend). But in that moment, it was clear that owning the house was no longer adding value to my life. It had become an obstacle to what I wanted to do next—travel and teach now that *Unstuff Your Life!* was published.

It's important to remember that my family and friends love me deeply when I tell you that the amount of resistance and pushback I got when I announced my plans was intense and relentless.

"You poured your blood, sweat, and tears into that house!"

"How can you sell it? It's so *you!*"

"You're joking right?! I could never imagine doing what you're doing."

And that was the bottom line.

Because they couldn't conceive of doing it, it must be wrong or foolish or a mistake for me to do it.

Their responses fed every one of my own doubts and fears.

Maybe they were right. Maybe I couldn't trust my ability to make smart choices for myself, financial or otherwise. And from there it was easy to identify every other mistake I had ever made in my life and draw a line straight through all of them to end up right where I was then.

They were trying to be supportive but, as we all know, when feedback is filtered through someone else's lens, it more often comes out sounding like criticism rather than support.

It took a tremendous amount of effort and patience to repeatedly explain why this was the right choice for me and how it completely aligned with my values. Having a similar conversation many times was hard work and emotionally expensive.

Maybe you can relate to being told you're being supported when it really feels like you're being negatively judged? And how, long after the initial event has occurred, something seemingly unrelated will kick up the same flush of shame or doubt as if no time had passed at all? Suddenly you find yourself having a conversation with yourself where you are both the attacker and the victim.

Whether it's about the clock or clutter, neutralizing that kind of self-talk is essential if we're going to reclaim our time and our lives.

And while it may require some serious effort to get rid of it, "a problem well-stated is a problem half-solved."[40]

I'm a firm believer in returning that noise to the source—if the person is still alive, you can do that directly. If they are no longer here, indirectly will have to be okay.

Just like the practice of removing the word "because" from your vocabulary, you do not need to justify your choices.

If there are consequences to the choices you've made, own them. That's the only price you have to pay for wanting what you want.

Here are some other questions to ask while prioritizing and laying out your days on your calendar:

- Does this have to be done today?
- Does this have to be done by me?
- Is this a step in a larger project or a one-off?
- Is there something more important I need to do first?
- Does this get me closer to my goals? If so, how?

TIME TRIAGE

Because there is not enough time to do everything in the world, you're going to have to get comfortable with "time triage" and making choices—otherwise you still won't be able to do everything *and* you'll be frustrated every time you crash into that reality.

Time triage is the practice of being real with yourself about how long things take, what's possible, and what you have to give up in order to do other things that matter more to you.

To minimize the sting of time triage, follow these steps:

1. Get as efficient as you can be with recurring tasks—that will buy you back some time you can redistribute to other activities.
2. Automate everything that doesn't require a human touch.
3. Delegate anything and everything you can afford to.
4. Don't let perfectionism keep you from letting good enough be enough.
5. When making a difficult decision, focus on what you're gaining rather than on what you're giving up.

A LAST PLUG FOR PARETO

Once you've identified the 20 percent of your work that delivers if not 80 percent then a significant percentage of your best and desired results, why not just double down on that? By doing 20 percent more of those tasks, you've essentially achieved an 80 percent increase. You're now getting a 160 percent return on a 40 percent investment of your time.

Even if you did nothing for the remaining 60 percent of your day, you've effectively doubled your output. Seems an easy way to turbo-charge your results, right?

THE BOTTOM LINE

You can't make strategic plans without data, so resist any stories about not being good at math or feeling like a robot. The data needed to plan and schedule can be gathered using an ordinary stopwatch. You just need to measure how long things actually take.

Remember that you are the most important person to you. If you don't value your time, no one else will.

Caring for yourself doesn't make you selfish, and is required if you're going to get anything done that matters to you. Bonus—it allows you to more effectively serve others, too.

"Trust your gut" on what to do, but use math and strategy—that is, planning—to figure out how and when to do it.

When everything is precious, nothing is precious—you've got to be able to distinguish between things if you're going to effectively prioritize.

When in doubt, use your values to prioritize. Don't guess or people-please. And utilize the concept of time triage as an antidote to anxiety or feeling overwhelmed.

ADHD or not, pay attention to when you disappear or lose focus. And remember that your calendar is your time bible—so get religious about time the smart way.

You don't need a fancy or expensive system like a Franklin Planner or Day Runner. The calendar built into your smartphone or bundled with your computer's operating system will work fine. Simple is better. The important thing is to make your calendar your map for how you'll move through your days, weeks, months, and years.

Important events and activities will not "just happen" because you want them to. But going too far in the other direction makes you rigid and unyielding. The middle way allows you to plan while remaining curious, willing, and flexible.

No plan should be so constrictive that it feels like a straitjacket or a life sentence.

CHANNELING YOUR INNER DATA NERD
Set a timer for 15 minutes and figure out what your highest-value 20 percent is. Then add that information to your values to use when prioritizing.

Time yourself for seven days and really study how long things take to do. Be gentle but firm with yourself until you have a clear understanding of how quickly or slowly you work. Don't judge; just observe and record.

Use the steps for planning laid out in this chapter to start building out your calendar. Do a day or a week at a time until you feel a degree of comfort and even mastery over scheduling.

CHAPTER RECAP

Learning how to plan properly is one of the keys to successfully managing your time.

Planning your days ahead of time will not turn you into a robot. You are still in charge of yourself and your calendar. Planning is also not the death of spontaneity. Rather than killing spontaneity, planning makes it possible without sacrificing your goals. And serendipity and planning aren't mutually exclusive. Magic can happen inside a plan; it just doesn't replace the plan.

Planning lets you map out what you're going to do on any given day, at what time, and in what order to achieve your goals as quickly and efficiently as possible.

If something unexpected comes up, you can rearrange the plan or even pause the plan. Planning is the alternative to and antidote for "flying by the seat of your pants" or "shooting first and asking questions later."

Whenever you compare your time management with the way others manage their time and you feel like you're losing the race, it's helpful to remember that 1) it's not a race, and 2) we all get the exact same number of hours in a week: 168. How well we use them is up to us. Part of that equation depends on your willingness and ability to plan.

Other people might accomplish more than you do in your 168 hours . . . this week. The only thing we know for sure is that it's not because they have more time. It could be because they are using those hours more strategically. And what's the secret behind their strategy? I'm willing to bet it's planning.

Chances are you have more time than you think you do. It's not always obvious where the time goes. Big chunks of time are often easier to track down than the 5- and 10-minute "little" blips that are actually robbing you senseless. By themselves, they seem inconsequential and are easy to discount. But over time, those 5- and 10-minute bits will add up to one year or more lost for the average person.

You also can't manage what you don't measure. The Pareto Principle suggests that 80 percent of your desired results come from the top or most effective 20 percent of your efforts. Figuring out your most impactful 20 percent and focusing on doing more of that will shift your behavior from merely busy to highly effective and impactful.

The math is simple here. If 20 percent of your best efforts are responsible for 80 percent of your optimal results, by just doing 20 percent more of those tasks, you've achieved an 80 percent increase in your output. You're now getting a 160 percent return on a 40 percent investment of your time. Even if you did nothing else that day, you've effectively doubled your performance. That's pretty impressive.

Another benefit of planning is that it reduces stress and unnecessary demands on our brains. Human brains did not evolve to hold large volumes of data indefinitely. They're designed for quick and nimble fight-or-flight responses.

So if in the past you often assumed you'd remember important details but then struggled to recall them when you needed them, all that time you were struggling was wasted time. To prevent that in the future, conserve your energy and bandwidth by *writing them down* instead, then filing them using the Organizational Triangle. That way, like-with-like information will be stored with its siblings and you'll be able to find it in 30 seconds or less. Properly labeling and filing this information also eliminates rewriting the same lists over and over again as you try to document everything you've been holding in your head.

HOW TO START PLANNING EFFECTIVELY

ESTABLISH TIMES FOR EACH TASK

You can't make an appointment with yourself if you don't know how long it takes to do something.

We already talked in Chapter 2 about using your stopwatch (or the stopwatch function on a digital timer) to capture how long you actually spend doing a task.

While this is less important for tasks you'll only do once, it's useful to understand how fast or slow you typically work, regardless of what you're working on.

Once you have that data, use it when laying out your day so you don't under- or overestimate how long to allow for each task.

And remember that even though you may not finish the entire task in the time allotted, the goal was merely to work on the task uninterrupted for the duration of that block of time. Of course, you should find an appropriate place to pause the task if it's unfinished so you can easily pick up where you left off. When writing, I change the text color to red to indicate where I need to start the next time.

Trust that each block of time will move the task forward. And when you are finished, you'll have additional data on what you can reasonably expect to accomplish in each of the individual blocks of time that it took you to complete the entire task.

TO-DO LISTS

These are just lists of things you could do until any of the items on a list becomes important enough for you to invest your time and energy in doing it.

Think of a to-do list as a parking lot where you can dump everything out of your brain and look at what you've been thinking of, what you want to do, what you need to do, and what you don't want to forget to do.

Once you've written everything down, start moving individual tasks into like-with-like categories called time buckets.

TIME BUCKETS

Regardless of how other people define time buckets, here we're using the term to mean time categories. By thinking of them as buckets rather than just categories, you can now drop like-with-like tasks into each bucket as a way of grouping them together. For visual thinkers, a list imposes a visual hierarchy as you add each task to it.

Better to gather them all in one place before you begin to prioritize within each bucket. Only then will you want to evaluate which tasks are more important and which may be subordinate or dependent on others, and rank them accordingly.

Your time buckets will be unique to you, but here are two starter sets to get your juices flowing. Note they are listed in alphabetical order, not in order of significance. You can choose to arrange them in any way that best serves you.

You can find examples of my and some of my clients' time buckets at cbobbook.com/planning.

WORK

Admin & Clerical, WORK,
  including Sorting & Filing
Advertising
Business Development
Client Services

Errands
Financial
Marketing
Planning
Professional Development

Project 1   Research
Project 2   Volunteering & Community
Public Relations   Other

LIFE

Admin & Clerical, LIFE,   Home Maintenance
  including Sorting & Filing   Medical
Creative Expression   Organizing & Simplifying
Errands   Project 1
Education   Self-Care
Financial   Self-Development
Friends & Family   Spiritual Practices
Giving Back   Volunteering & Community
Health & Fitness   Other

Once you have your list of time buckets, this is how you will work with them:

1. First gather all your to-do lists—you may have only one or, like many people, you may have multiple lists floating around.
2. If you have multiple lists and they are already category- or time bucket–specific, move the contents of an entire list right into its corresponding bucket.
3. If you have multiple lists and they are not category-specific, review and harvest items one by one from these lists, crossing out any duplicate tasks as you come across them.
4. As soon as any list is empty, delete it or toss it rather than creating more clutter and saving it "just in case."
5. Once all your current to-dos are in their appropriate buckets, assign times to as many as you can based on your noble experiment of timing your tasks.
6. When you've quantified as many tasks as you can, start to prioritize the tasks in their buckets (levels 1, 2, 3, etc.).

7. When all the tasks are prioritized inside their buckets, you can prioritize the buckets themselves.

NOTE: If you are working with your time buckets digitally, save your work often. Also, use your values and any external deadlines to inform the level of priority you're assigning in Steps 6 and 7.

CALENDAR

Once you have your to-dos sorted into their proper time buckets *and* have them quantified and prioritized according to your values and any deadlines, it's time to use your calendar and plan.

Your calendar becomes the visual representation of your plan. Like any other map, you just have to follow it to get to your destination.

If you're thorough in your planning, your calendar will reflect all the research, thinking, and deciding you've done prior to scheduling any task.

As you lay out your calendar, you should first load any recurring high-value commitments you have into your calendar—if all you know right now is the categories (or time buckets) of those commitments, you can fill in the details of which specific tasks and activities you'll do closer to the date.

For example, I block out two hours at a time for writing and then fill in which specific writing project I'll be working on either at the beginning of the week or sometimes as late as that morning. The important thing is to have time set aside *for* writing.

Look in your buckets for 1- and 2-level tasks that are one-offs, and schedule them around your recurring time blocks.

Think like a time hacker and look for any tasks or series of tasks you can streamline to save time. Recurring tasks give you the greatest return on this kind of hacking. The more observant of and familiar with each task or group of tasks you are, the easier and faster it will be to identify which parts can be eliminated, trimmed, or sped up.

While you can't multitask, you can pivot between tasks smoothly and quickly, particularly tasks that have something in common. Consider this when looking for a more efficient flow to how you're mapping out your day.

When it comes to running errands, schedule them the way delivery services do—go to the farthest location first and work your way back home with each subsequent stop.

If you still have time available in your calendar after you've loaded in your recurring and one-off level 1 and 2 tasks, and you can reasonably fit more in, go back to your buckets and find any level-3 to-dos. Fold those into your day and week thoughtfully.

It's always better, in the beginning, to leave more time open in your calendar than you think you need. That way, you can respond to the unexpected, as well as to your energy levels and ability to focus as the day evolves. It's much easier to add things at the last moment than it is to remove or postpone them, especially if they involve other people. In those cases, you have to consider the impact of the disruption on you and everyone else.

Anything that is a level 4 or 5 priority should be delegated or removed from your buckets completely.

There is not enough time to do everything in the world, so get comfortable with the concept of "time triage." It's the practice of being honest with yourself about how long things take, what's possible, and what you will have to sacrifice to allow enough time for activities that matter more to you.

To minimize the sting of time triage, follow these steps:

1. Adjust your attitude as needed so the concept of letting some things go in the service of doing other things sits well enough with you. You don't have to love it but you do need to accept it.
2. Get as efficient as you can be with recurring tasks—that will buy you back some time that you can redistribute to other activities.
3. Automate everything that doesn't require a human touch.
4. Delegate anything and everything you can afford to.
5. Don't let perfectionism keep you from letting good enough be enough.
6. When making a difficult decision, focus on what you're gaining rather than on what you're giving up—this usually softens any disappointment.

Chapter 8
Email

"I didn't have time to write you a short letter,
so I wrote you a long one."
Mark Twain

"With email, the old postcard rule applies.
Nobody else is supposed to read it, but you'd be
a fool to write anything private in one."
Judith Martin

Email is everywhere. It's a brilliant invention and it also kind of sucks. It's plagued by spam, but it's free. It's useful when we don't abuse it.

And since it's not going away any time soon, let's figure out how to use it effectively with the least friction possible.

As a means of communication, email has become the preferred method for a sizable chunk of the world's businesses.

It's less intrusive than a phone call, more robust than a text message, and much, much faster than sending a snail-mail letter.

The speed of email was a game changer for modern connectivity, but it's become a double-edged sword. Given how fast it arrives, it's easy to see why we think we need to respond just as quickly.

But just because email pings almost instantly from server to server, landing in our inboxes at all hours, 24/7/365—unless it's snagged by any number of spam filters—does not mean that it requires or deserves your immediate attention.

With any time thief, it's important to blow up the lie that immediacy equals importance.

It may be radical to establish your own rules for how and when you use email, but the alternative means you are at the mercy of an app. That seems very Big Brother to me.

And if you're muttering that I just don't understand the way *you* use email, I bet I do.

Of course, if your entire job is answering emails—meaning, you're in customer service at a help desk or managing someone else's inbox—then during working hours, there may be specific requirements about email turnaround time. Your employer may dictate the timing of when and, to some degree, how you reply. They may not get so granular as to dictate how you organize your email, which emails you prioritize, and which you pass along.

Either way, unless instructed otherwise, just because email arrives at the speed of light does not mean you have to read or reply to it right away.

This chapter will teach you to create a set of intentional rules defining how and when you use email.

I'm sure experts like my friend Thomas Farley, Mr. Manners, or Judith Martin, Miss Manners, can share some accepted rules around how quickly you need to reply before being considered rude, but there is a lot of leeway between that and firing off a reply regardless of sender, content, or need.

For fun, let's imagine a physical mail carrier coming to your house 100+ times a day to drop another piece of mail in your inbox—that's the average number of emails we receive each day. A lot of steps for them, certainly—but you wouldn't meet them at the door each time, right?

You'd let the mail accumulate and, a few times a day at most, you'd retrieve it and sort through it before it turned into a big mess.

Now imagine that you *did* meet that mail carrier at the door. Every. Single. Time. You'd never get anything done or even leave your house.

That's what happens when you live inside your email inbox.

If you can't free yourself from the slightly insane notion that you need to drop everything and answer every ding and ping of an incoming email, you'll always feel trapped and controlled by a machine and you'll be helpless to take control of your time.

THE PROBLEMS WITH NOT HAVING AN EMAIL PROTOCOL

Email has some great qualities, including its speed and accessibility. It equalizes communication beyond geography—around the corner or across the globe, it gets there just as fast.

Unlike a handwritten letter, we can enlarge or shrink our view of it with the push of a button. We can attach files to it and we can automate its arrival, sorting it into folders for later viewing or storing. We can delete it instantly, and sift through it just as quickly.

And unlike a phone call that might intrude at odd hours, we can fire off an email whenever it's convenient for us, knowing its arrival won't disturb the recipient and the message will just wait until they choose to read it.

Email can also be a useful note-taking device on the go—though not, as we'll see, a great tool for keeping to-do lists.

What email is *not* is an urgent demand for our attention and a promise we will always be on high alert.

Of course, email has other problems, too.

- It's everywhere. Email is probably on all of your devices— smartwatch, smartphone, tablet, laptop, desktop, etc. It can feel inescapable.
- It never stops coming. It's like that postal carrier constantly at your door, day and night.
- There aren't any universal rules for how and when to use it— you have to establish your own.
- It's used for everything—from correspondence you want and subscriptions you've signed up for, to log-in credentials for websites and unsolicited spam.
- Without a system, you may be storing everything in a single inbox—work and personal messages, newsletters, sales flyers, event announcements, and again spam.
- Since you probably use it for work and personal correspondence, boundaries may be hard to set up and keep. You might hop on to quickly check your personal email and get hooked by a work email instead.
- Many people use their inbox as a tickler file and a filing cabinet, hoping that by leaving everything there, they'll remember to do (or answer) an email the next time they log on.
- Email begets email. The more, and more quickly, you reply to incoming messages, the more emails you get in return, just as fast. Like Whac-A-Mole, this is a game that never ends . . . unless you end it.

It's up to you to decide how and when you want to use email and then share those decisions, or rules of engagement, with everyone you regularly communicate with. Otherwise, they'll assume you use email the way they do.

What is an acceptable turnaround time for each type of email—from a friend, boss, colleague, family, stranger—and when do you want to check email, how often, and for how long? Those parameters are a great place to start deciding how and when you'll use it.

CONSEQUENCES OF NOT HAVING EMAIL GUIDELINES

Until you set up your guidelines for using email, you may suffer any of these consequences:

- Constant or frequent distraction and interruption
- Limited—or nonexistent—boundaries between work life and personal life
- Wasted time when keyword searches fail to accurately sort overcrowded inboxes
- Wasted time when a key piece of missed information causes a delay in starting or finishing a task or project
- Wasted time when piecemeal info requires repeated clarifications instead of covering all details in one quick real-time call
- Wasted time spent discussing tasks instead of executing them
- Lost information when servers erroneously delete messages or humans push the wrong buttons or swipe too fast
- Wasted time and lost information when emails and attachments are jumbled together in the digital equivalent of a junk drawer

- Frustration when you've asked the same question three times but it keeps getting overlooked because it's buried in a long thread
- Other communication misunderstandings and confusion stemming from the following issues:
  - Not everyone is a native speaker of your first language
  - Even native speakers have different interpretations of what words mean
  - We often leave out context, assuming everyone can easily follow our line of thinking
  - For average writers, email requires exceptional effort to communicate with any nuance or subtlety
  - It's difficult to convey and interpret tone—was the email intended to be rude or short, or was it just not reviewed for tone first?

WHY YOU NEED A SYSTEM FOR EMAIL

Using email without a system designed by and for you will fracture your attention and impact your productivity.

Consider these stats: the average person checks their email at least 15 times per day. That works out to every 32 minutes—and many of us are checking it far more often than twice an hour.[41]

All that checking and rechecking takes a substantial toll, and not just the time lost recovering from all the interruptions. For a refresher on interruptions, see Chapter 4.

Studies show that when people check their email just three times a day, they have less stress, complete more important work, and feel more accomplished at the end of the workday.[42]

Even the *Harvard Business Review* study cited above found that no one really expects a reply every 30 minutes.[43]

When you reply to every email the moment it hits your inbox, you're training your colleagues, clients, and yourself that this is the norm. That creates or reinforces expectations. It also limits your ability to focus on anything *other than* email for extended periods of time.

You're creating a habit that doesn't serve you. That habit becomes harder to change or resist the more you get rewarded for doing it. The rush you get from seeing new messages actually alters your brain chemistry.[44]

And the way many people use their inbox as a giant catchall for reference material, work requirements, and to-dos is fundamentally broken.

Your inbox was never intended to function as a file folder. It's a general holding tank by design. Regardless of how robust AI search becomes, it will only ever be as effective as the person searching. That means if you're relying on search to compensate for your absence of a filing system, you need to be really accurate in your key word usage.

So structure and a system for filing important emails will save time and put you in control of your email experience.

CREATING A SIMPLE SYSTEM FOR USING EMAIL

Fixing our relationship with email requires a two-pronged approach: leveraging technology and adjusting our mindset.

For too many of us, the always-on electronic tether that is social media and email creates a false sense of intimacy and connection. That leads to feeling like you're always visible, which is bad for the psyche and feeds any people-pleasing tendencies, too.

What was once an unconscious habit of absently checking email has morphed into a compulsive reflex, like a nervous tic.

I understand wanting to be the person who responds early and often to email because you want to be liked and needed and judged favorably. The problem is that you can't please everyone all the time, so this is a contest you cannot win.

Another problem may be your own limiting beliefs that define how much freedom you will let yourself have.

"I'd love to check my email less," you might say, "but it just isn't possible because of X, Y, or Z."

That's almost always one of your 200 lies, so examine it carefully to see if it's really true.

I used to check email anytime I had a few minutes—at the doctor's office, in line at the grocery store, while waiting to meet someone. I thought I was being strategic with those few minutes of unstructured time.

Once I broke the habit of constantly dipping into my inbox, I quickly realized that I got very few emails that actually mattered and required my attention. That discovery was quite liberating.

Even more interesting was that I seldom needed the full 30 minutes I had blocked out on my calendar to write and respond to email. I trimmed that back to 15 minutes, which still left me plenty of time to get back to people. Could it really be that the bulk of the emails coming in were inconsequential? In my experience the answer was and is *yes*.

That led me to start wholesale unsubscribing from all kinds of lists I had joined. I wasn't reading those emails anyway, so they were just digital clutter. Besides, any time I want to opt back in, any of those services and thought leaders will be happy to add me to their lists.

So if you want to take your life back from email, follow these new rules.

They're customizable based on your preferences and circumstances, of course, but keep an eye out for those 200 lies. They tend to sneak in the back door with thoughts like "That would never work for *me*" or "My boss would never go for that."

If you've never asked for permission or forgiveness, then you're just making up stories. When in doubt, ask and confirm—don't imagine and catastrophize.

These new rules might feel uncomfortable the first few times you try them out, but once they become habits, you'll never look back.

PICK TWO OR THREE TIMES PER DAY TO CHECK EMAIL

You could check once in the morning to see if there's anything that is urgent or requires a schedule change for the day.

Then check in the late afternoon—leaving you enough time to reply before shutting down email for the day.

If that seems too radical, you can check a third time, before or after lunch.

Set up recurring appointments on your calendar for checking and replying, and then stick to them. Time yourself to see if you need all the time you've set aside for email—you may not.

Watch out for "killing time" in queues, waiting rooms, etc., like I used to do. You'll tell yourself there's no harm in looking—even compounding the lie by claiming you're being strategic with your time. I've been there, too.

Instead, read a book, meditate, return a call—and keep your nose out of your email. An innocent peek here and there is how new habits are broken and compulsive behavior is rewarded.

CHECK EMAIL ONLY WHEN YOU CAN READ AND RESPOND

We've all been there, checking email as soon as you open your eyes in the morning, just before bed, or on a family vacation. What follows is pointless stress when you don't have enough time to write a thoughtful reply to what you've just read.

At best, you've wasted the time it took to read the email. You'll have to read it again when you can reply. At worst, you are now upset by what you've read and can't focus on anything else because you're so agitated.

When that intrusion happens, you may get more upset and even direct that anger at the sender. But *you* are actually responsible for that upset—not the sender.

Your feelings about the content of the email are distinct from your feelings about your feelings, but they easily get mashed up in the moment.

This is where personal responsibility for our choices is so powerful. And while it sucks to admit it, the upset belongs to us.

If there was any chance a hungry lion was waiting behind a closed door, wouldn't you think twice before flinging it open?

Treat your inbox and your own well-being with the same caution and care.

NEVER SEND AN EMAIL WHEN YOU'RE UPSET

If you have a negative emotional response to an email, it may be therapeutic to aggressively bang out your wounded, snarky response. Just don't hit Send.

Give yourself at least 24 hours to read and review any potentially explosive emails before sending them out.

CHECK EMAIL ON DEMAND AND DISABLE AUTOMATIC CHECKING

When you're not actively reading and answering email, close down your email program and turn off automatic mail checking.

You're not saving any time by having your email app downloading messages in the background.

STOP USING EMAIL FOR INTERNAL COMMUNICATION

This mostly applies to businesses but can be used by everyone. This one tip shaved 30 percent off a client's total time on internal communications. That led to their best performing quarter in 2021, with each month improving over the last, until they had doubled their revenue in just 90 days.

Instant messaging apps like Slack are far faster and more efficient for keeping conversation threads tidy and concise. They also help reduce the number of emails you get during the day, and force any back-and-forth to stay short and to the point.

You can manually tag anyone you want to communicate with in any thread at any time. That ends the glut of .cc and .bcc messages flooding inboxes and allows you to target your communication to only the people who need to know or respond.

SILENCE/MUTE ALL EMAIL NOTIFICATIONS, INCLUDING BADGES

Those numbers popping up on your email app's icon or the pings you get when a new email comes in are clearly doing their jobs of interrupting you and pulling your attention away from whatever you were doing—so turn them off. You don't need to be alerted as new emails arrive.

Instead, stick with the two or three time slots per day to check email as outlined above. If these are on your calendar, you'll never need a ding or ping again.

Turning off your notifications is the best way to break the habit of compulsive email checking.

SET UP FILTERS TO AUTOSORT YOUR INCOMING EMAILS

When your inbox is overstuffed, things fall through the cracks. Establishing filters that direct your email before you ever see it is like automated triage. Let AI do the work so you don't have to.

FYI, rules and filters are the same thing—some email apps call them rules, others call them filters.

Whatever they're called, they redirect incoming email into any subfolder you've set up in advance before they land in your inbox.

Those folders should be based on the categories or types of email you regularly get. This is Like with Like for email.

The filters can be based on just about anything, from very granular choices like an individual sender's email address, to broader parameters like a company's overall domain. You can filter by commonly used keywords, full subject lines, dates, etc.

When you use filters to presort your email, any subfolder with new messages in it will have a numeric indicator on that folder reflecting the number of unread emails inside. That should resolve any concerns that you'll miss an important message from a client and other high-priority sender.

Once you start using filters, you'll discover how few emails actually need or deserve your attention and time.

To see an example of what my filters look like, visit cbobbook.com/email.

BUDGET ENOUGH TIME TO ANSWER EMAILS

Email that you have to answer comes in two flavors: One needs care and thought to write a nuanced reply. The other flavor is more mechanical, where you're answering a specific question or sharing information.

Many of the mechanical emails can be sent in just a minute or two, and even templated like your own version of FAQs. That way you don't have to retype the same information over and over again.

If you have an assistant, replying to the mechanical emails could also be delegated to them.

If you get a pretty even split of both flavors daily, set up two smaller blocks of time inside each of your email blocks so you can move through the mechanical ones quickly.

That will allow you enough time to craft any thoughtful replies without feeling rushed.

To figure out how long it takes *you* to write both kinds of emails, use your stopwatch to time a few of them, then use that data when budgeting time going forward.

Want to learn how to write a concise, direct email and avoid confusion? Check out the endnotes for an article by Kabir Sehgal in the *Harvard Business Review*.[45]

MAKE EMAILS EARN YOUR ATTENTION

While I never want to be rude, I learned a long time ago that just because an unsolicited email shows up in my inbox, it isn't automatically entitled to a reply.

I'm not talking about fan letters or people looking to genuinely connect with me. I'm talking about emails that, more often than not, are trying to sell me something that I didn't go looking for.

Add into the mix that some if not all of these emails are sent by AI bots and spammers phishing for a reply and you can quickly see what a colossal imposition it is to sift through these emails looking for anything of value.

Rather than spending my most precious resource replying to a stranger or a robot, I have my assistant set aside 15 minutes each day to scan for anything useful in my inbox and up to 30 minutes every week to quickly scroll through my Spam folder. More often than not, she doesn't find a single email that merits a response and so they are tossed in the trash immediately. For the rare email that does need a reply, I'll usually delegate drafting the initial reply to my assistant as well so she can vet the sender first.

AVOID CHECKING EMAIL AT YOUR MOST PRODUCTIVE TIME OF DAY

I write in the mornings when I'm freshest and at my sharpest. I don't even open my inbox until I've written for one hour. That's what works for me. What works best for you?

If you were a brain surgeon—and I get that answering emails is not equivalent to brain surgery—you wouldn't schedule an operation at the end of the day if you're dead on your feet by 3:00 p.m.

So pretend you *are* a brain surgeon. Schedule your highest-value activities as if they were surgeries and give them the time and attention they need. Then use your less productive times of the day to go through your emails.

REPLY WHEN NECESSARY

We've talked a lot about when *not* to answer an email. Here's one time when you should.

Many emails don't require a response, but some do—when they come from people you know or have a relationship with.

Even if the reply is just "no," "no, thanks," or "I can't," don't leave the sender hanging. Remember, the only thing better than good news is bad news fast.

If you don't have the answer or can't help, but you know someone who does or can, forward the email to that person and cc the sender *ASAP*. That way, you win, the sender wins, and you've taken yourself out of the loop.

DON'T USE YOUR INBOX AS A TO-DO LIST OR FILING CABINET
We went over this in the previous chapter, Poor Planning.

To-do lists are obsolete technology and should be replaced by time buckets, with all tasks quantified and ready to be pulled out from their buckets according to category and priority.

Just like physical clutter, emails sitting around in your inbox are digital clutter; they are just tiny electronic deferred decisions.

Be honest—given all the demands on your time, are you actually going to read a newsletter or promo email from three months ago? If it wasn't important enough to read when it first arrived, how relevant is that content now?

UPDATE SUBJECT LINES AND USE THEM STRATEGICALLY
Subject lines that do not accurately reflect what's in the email are a huge time waster. Regardless of whether you started the email thread or not, always update the subject line to reflect the current conversation, especially in a long thread that changes scope over time.

Make them clear, not cutesy—and remember you're not paying by the word. Use full sentences, actual words and complete thoughts. Avoid the use of text message abbreviations like "how r u," or "c u later." Even when you're writing to friends or family, using any sort of insider joke or slang can quickly become confusing and even inflammatory.

If you're worried about missing something time-sensitive, suggest senders include the words "URGENT" or "ACTION NEEDED" in their subject lines—then pay attention if they overuse this feature.

USE THE SUBJECT LINE AS THE MESSAGE AND END IT WITH EOM

When a piece of information needs fewer than 15 words to communicate it, make *it* the subject line.

Don't fluff or pad your correspondence—just write what you need to.

Then add these three letters, EOM, which tells the reader that this is the "end of (the) message." They don't have to waste time opening an empty message. This is particularly helpful on mobile devices when scrolling through subject lines to see what needs attention.

If you want some bonus points, use NRN after EOM to indicate "no reply needed."

You can see a real-time example of this at cbobbook.com/email.

READ THE ENTIRE THREAD BEFORE REPLYING

Some people fire off responses when they are "in their feelings" and not thinking clearly, right?

They joined the conversation late or they're distracted. They want to seem relevant so they jump in midstream, without knowing what the full conversation contains.

Please don't do this yourself.

We've got to learn to manage our emotions so we don't send hasty or premature emails. When that happens, there are all kinds of potential consequences.

Depending on your level of authority, you could send people off on a wild goose chase. You could reopen a contentious conversation that had already been resolved. Time will be wasted cleaning up any mess—all of which is unnecessary and avoidable.

Preventing any of this is simple. Move slowly, and thoroughly read the full thread before you send a reply.

MAKE YOUR COMMUNICATION PREFERENCES PUBLIC

Once you've decided when you'll check email and the turnaround time that people can expect, put that information in your email signature.

You can literally say, "I check my email three times a day: X, Y, and Z. Want to know why? Ask me the next time we talk."

If efficiency or productivity are part of your brand or job, this is a great way to hook your readers and make your signature work for you.

You can share these details with clients and colleagues, if you think it's necessary, so they can align their expectations with your behavior.

You can also include a phone number in your signature as an urgent alternative.

If people know how to reach you in an emergency, it should reduce everyone's anxiety over a possible missed email. Besides, how often is an email really that urgent?

THE BOTTOM LINE

Mindlessly, compulsively checking email steals your time.

End the tyranny of machines and get outside—and leave your phone behind.

For most of us, if we did something good for ourselves as often as we checked our email, we'd see some impressive results.

Book consistent times to check your email and then put the app to bed or shut it down. Turn off notifications and stop lurking in your inbox—chances are there are better things to read and better uses of your time.

Use any or all of the new rules listed above and you will easily regain one hour or more a day.

Remember, too, that the more email you send, the more you receive—so use email intentionally and as little as possible.

Let others know about any changes you're putting in place so they can adjust their expectations accordingly.

CHAPTER RECAP

Email is now everywhere, and it can be a blessing or a curse, depending on how we use it. Either way, do not get sucked into believing that immediacy = importance. It doesn't.

Email's arrival in your inbox does not equal an emergency or a crisis. With very few exceptions, you do not have to read or reply to it right away.

You get to decide how and when you will use email. It's also a good idea to share those parameters with everyone you regularly communicate with. Otherwise, they'll assume you use email the way they use email.

When you reply to every email the moment it arrives, you're training colleagues, clients, and yourself to believe that this is the norm. That creates or reinforces expectations and establishes a habit that doesn't serve you, which becomes harder to change or resist the more you get rewarded for doing it. It also limits your ability to focus on anything other than email for extended periods of time.

Consider this: the average person checks their email at least 15 times per day, or about every 32 minutes—and many of us check it far more often than twice an hour.

All that checking and rechecking takes a substantial toll, whether it's the time lost recovering from all those notifications (interruptions) or, more significantly, the loss of 10 IQ points, along with substantial mental energy and clarity as we task-switch in and out of our inboxes.

Studies show that when people check their email just three times a day, they have less stress, complete more important work, and feel they've accomplished more at the end of the workday.

Also, leaving all your email in your inbox is not an efficient way to work with email. That inbox was never intended to function as a filing cabinet. It's a loading zone, not a storage locker.

HOW TO USE EMAIL EFFICIENTLY

Here are 15 actions you can take and behaviors you can change that will revolutionize how and when you use email. By applying even three of them, you can easily net back an hour or more every day:

- Pick three times per day to check email.
- Check email only when you can read it and respond to it.
- You can write an email when you're upset, but never push send until you've calmed down.
- Disable automatic checking to only check email on demand.
- Stop using email for internal communication—switch to Slack, MS Teams, etc.
- Silence/mute all email notifications, including badges.
- Set up filters or rules to auto-sort your emails into designated subfolders.
- Block out time for email based on the time you'll need to reply—then adjust as needed.
- Make email earn your attention.
- Never check or answer email at your most productive time of day.
- Reply when necessary—impatient senders may continue to ping you until they get an answer.
- Don't treat your email inbox as a to-do list or a filing cabinet.
- Update subject lines any time the thread changes content or direction.
- For short messages, use the subject line as the entire message, ending it with EOM (end of message.)
- Read the entire thread before replying to avoid redundancy or embarrassment.
- Make your email and other communication preferences public.

Chapter 9
Meetings

"People who enjoy meetings should not
be in charge of anything."
Thomas Sowell

"There are two kinds of people: those who do the work
and those who take the credit. I always try to be in the
first group; there is much less competition."
Indira Gandhi

Most meetings are a waste of time.

They lack a clear purpose, a concise agenda, and a simple process for capturing and following up on next steps. They start off vague and go nowhere.

I've seen some meetings where the person in charge is terrified of making a unilateral decision, even if that's their job, so they drag the rest of the team into the room as cover. Then, when things go south, someone else takes the blame and the boss lives to see another day.

Brainstorming sessions with no process for sparking creativity are some of the worst offenders. Attendees are invited to throw random ideas at the wall, hoping something brilliant appears and then sticks. When it doesn't, everyone scratches their heads, wondering why so many talented people couldn't come up with a single good idea.

For a meeting to be successful, it needs an agenda. That could be to fix a problem; update an existing product, service, or project; launch a project; or create a brand-new product or service.

You don't have to be a math whiz to figure out how much time is lost in just one needless hour-long meeting. Take the 60 minutes that you wasted and multiply it by the number of people in the room—suddenly that hour becomes 5 or even 10 hours gone.

And how many times does that happen each week?

There are many more efficient—and more easily documented—ways to update and collaborate with your team.

Messaging apps like Slack and project management apps like Asana can keep everyone on the same page—tracking progress, gathering opinions, assigning tasks, and distributing updates without pulling the whole company into the conference room or onto Zoom.

So while we can't eliminate *all* meetings, let's make sure that when we do meet, we get something useful done quickly and on time.

PROBLEMS WITH MEETINGS

This section is organized into three sections—structure, people, and purpose—so you can home in on your biggest meeting challenges first.

STRUCTURE
Let's start with a typical meeting's structure—or lack thereof.

You've got to have a written agenda, someone to open and close the meeting on time, and someone to run the meeting, including holding everyone accountable during the meeting.

One bad meeting can disrupt an entire workday. A culture of useless meetings can eat away at a multinational corporation.[46]

Most meetings are also much longer than they need to be.

No meeting should ever be longer than 60 minutes, max, and most should be under 30 minutes. Over 80 percent of attendees start to lose focus after 30 minutes.[47]

And then there's the lack of takeaways, follow-up, and follow-through.

Follow-up tasks often fall through the cracks or require a meeting of their own to get back on track.

What's worse, when follow-up meetings are scheduled, the first 15 minutes are often wasted reviewing what was covered in the last meeting and "reminding" people of what they agreed to do previously.

Back-to-back meetings create bottlenecks and are responsible for increased stress and an inability to stay focused during the meetings. Almost 40 percent of workers report outright exhaustion as a result, according to a recent Microsoft study.[48]

When you run from one meeting to another, even if you make it on time, you'll still be thinking about the last meeting as you roll into the next one. Your brain needs time to transition and get up to speed.

You'll forget what you just committed to in the last meeting or be so distracted by debriefing yourself that you won't be paying full attention in the current meeting—either way, both meetings are impacted.

PEOPLE

Meetings don't exist without people—and, no disrespect to *Hamilton*, a room can only be "where it happens" if the right people are there, on time and ready to work.

It's sloppy and unprofessional when anyone shows up late—and that's compounded the minute they offer an excuse for being tardy.

You're sending a clear message that people's time doesn't matter and neither do results when you tolerate or condone showing up late, running long, or both. Eventually, that attitude will be reflected in the overall company's culture as well.

When everyone isn't prepared *before* the meeting, there's little value in proceeding.

While a rehearsal is not a traditional kind of meeting, I remember the first time I heard director Dr. James Rapport ("Daddy Bear" to his students) tell an assembled cast that he expected us to arrive at every rehearsal with a "full lunch box." That meant reviewing the scenes, studying our lines, and creatively exploring the text in advance—so we were fully prepared before we ever got on stage.

If, during the meeting, attendees are fumbling to find their agenda or other docs, or share their screen, or they are otherwise unprepared, the energy and focus in the room will rapidly splinter and fade.

Sometimes it's hard to get the right people even in the room. Key decision makers may think they don't need to attend when the guest list is too long.

At other times, they won't be included due to human error, personality conflicts, or office politics. And occasionally, a key person can't attend for reasons beyond anyone's control, like a personal emergency or last-minute travel changes.

When a day is full of meetings, there's little time to get actual work done.

Over 90 percent of workers complain that meetings are costly and un-productive, creating more work and more stress as deadlines pile up.[49] Meetings make your task list longer, but not necessarily any clearer.

By comparison, workers report feeling less stressed by day-to-day work when they know who is doing what, by when, and what the result should be.

PURPOSE

A clear agenda does two things: it provides a structure and outlines the purpose.

There is no reason to ever have a meeting without a written agenda—none. Be wary of anyone who says, "Let's just get together and we'll figure it out then." Usually nothing gets figured out because no one's even sure why they're there.

The costs to businesses each year for ineffective meetings are staggering—$399 billion in the US alone.[50]

And recurring meetings are especially guilty of waste, especially when nothing significant has occurred since the last meeting.

BETTER MEETINGS START WITH YOUR CULTURE

If you want to improve the quality of meetings at work, look at your company culture first. Is it supportive of making changes to improve efficiency and reduce friction?

Does it reward ingenuity and innovation or does it subtly shame or shut down anyone who veers from the status quo?

I don't care how many inspirational posters you have in the break room or how great the coffee and snacks are—how do people function there?

Is there a feeling that anything is possible if it's the best choice for the company and its workers? Or is there an undercurrent of complacency and resistance to change?

Are suggestions met with "but this is how we've always done it"?

If you are a decision maker and want to save time, boost morale, and see your employees claim ownership over their work and their fulfillment, start by ensuring your culture is healthy and dynamic.

Then do not schedule a new meeting until you're confident it is justified.

Next, make any structural changes needed for how, when, and where they are held.

If you are not in management but are committed to your own growth and development, step up and help push the culture in the direction it needs to go.

Work alone if necessary, and with colleagues when possible, to move the organization forward so that everyone's time is valued and meetings only happen when they are absolutely necessary.

Whether you're an owner, management, or rank and file, you are still a stakeholder. As such, check your headspace to see if and where you've grown ambivalent, lazy, or resentful.

Get your head back in the game and elevate your company's experience of meetings.

So often when I am teaching government employees at the Fed, state or local level, participants will throw up their hands and say, "I'm just a cog in a huge, immovable machine. I have zero influence. What can I do?"

And I remind them that when they take responsibility for *everything* in their life, even a dysfunctional work culture, their personal power grows and they feel in greater control of their time and life.

I could write a whole book on workplace culture but, for now, let's stay focused on meetings.

HOW TO BUILD A PERFECT MEETING

Once you've addressed or at least begun to work on your company's culture, you can dig into improving the meetings there.

Not every meeting will be perfect in its outcome, but every meeting can be perfect in its design.

When a meeting's structure and purpose are clear and concise, everyone is free to be creative and fully present for whatever arises—and free to focus on *why* they're there in the first place.

Perfect meetings have a recipe, and here it is:

- Only the people who need to be there, who have something to contribute, should be invited and attending. Don't pad the room with supporters, fans, or dead weight.
- Send the agenda 72 hours ahead, if you can. At a minimum, it must be in people's hands 24 hours before you meet. Otherwise, people are spitballing during the meeting and you are not getting their best work.
- Be sure to attach any relevant resource materials to the agenda.
- 48 hours before the meeting takes place, conduct a roll call and make sure the right people have been invited. Use AI or other automation, email, or calls to confirm RSVPs and attendance.

- If a key person can't make it and they are critical to the meeting's success, reschedule to a time when everyone can be there. It is less expensive, time- and money-wise, to regroup than to plow ahead and then repeat the exact same meeting when the pivotal person can rejoin.
- Every confirmed attendee should know the answers to these questions before they walk in the room:
  - Who's calling for the meeting?
  - Who's running the meeting?
  - Who else is attending?
  - How long is the meeting?
  - Where is the meeting being held?
  - Is it mandatory that I be there?
  - If my attendance is not mandatory, how will I add value by attending?
- Make sure the purpose of the meeting is spelled out in the invite, ideally in one sentence: Why are we meeting? What do we need to complete during the allotted time?
- Set time limits for every agenda item. This reduces the impact of people who repeat themselves or echo a point already made. Time limits keep the conversation laser-focused.
- Clarify desired outcomes and assign roles in the agenda. Every meeting should have a timekeeper, an agenda keeper, a note taker, and a project manager to follow up on assigned tasks. These can be different people or the same person; what's important is that everyone knows who's doing what and what they are accountable for.
- Start meetings on time and ensure everyone sticks to the time limits set for each topic on the agenda.
- If you're not done with a point when the time runs out, table that discussion. It can become the subject of its own meeting or old business at the next meeting.
- Appoint a meeting "project manager" to assign or record all action items, deliverables, and timelines, and get verbal

confirmation before the meeting is over that everything is understood and agreed upon.

- No one should leave the meeting unclear about next steps or who is responsible for them and by when.
- Never book back-to-back meetings. Always leave time before and after to shake off the last meeting and get ready for the next meeting. Brain science proves a small buffer between meetings reduces stress and improves focus. This also prevents people from running into your meeting late from a previous meeting.
- Within 24 hours after the meeting, send a concise, thorough recap to all attendees or publish the notes on a shared app, server, or drive. Send them also to anyone who wasn't there but who needs to be in the loop, or alert them on where to find the published notes.
- Debrief yourself. The end of the meeting is not the end of the meeting. It's great that the project manager is handing out action items—you still need to integrate them into your calendar or to-do lists. Give yourself at least 15 minutes to update your calendar and to-do lists, read and revise any notes, and digest major takeaways and their implications.
- Engage any managers needed to ensure all assigned tasks get done by their due dates.

Want to up your game a few notches and cover a ton of ground as quickly as possible? Here's a bonus item for you.

- Make attendees stand. This has a few benefits: It's harder for people to "multitask," meaning check out mentally or audit the meeting while checking email, texting, or reading unrelated materials. It also ensures that no one gets so comfortable that they can't stay awake or on task.

Will every meeting run smoothly? No—shit happens.

Despite your best efforts, key people will be late or absent. Some agenda items will run long. You might discover that you met for the wrong purpose or are solving the wrong problem.

Again, the point isn't perfection in the meeting's outcome—although it's always great when magic happens.

By getting the structure and flow as close to perfect as you can, you allow everyone attending to let their guard down and dig in.

No one will waste energy stressing about what else they could be doing rather than suffering through another disorganized, unfocused meeting.

For a sample agenda template and other meeting tools, visit cbobbook. com/meetings.

SCHEDULING REMOTE MEETINGS STRADDLING TIME ZONES

As remote work shifts and evolves, you may be quite far geographically from others on the team. Depending on role, culture, and other factors, you may feel pressure to say yes to every meeting you're invited to.

Additionally, it might be hard to avoid or say no to meetings scheduled outside of your regular working hours.

Be clear about why you can't work every hour of the day across all time zones, even if it seems obvious, and then offer a few alternatives. Just like in improv theater, it's always better to say "yes, and . . ." than just saying no.

Take advantage of apps like Slack that display each team member's time zone. Click on "View Profile" and it will show you what time it is where anyone lives.

If you've got to set up meetings straddling distant time zones, here are some guidelines:

- Make it fair: When teams are separated by oceans (for example, San Francisco and Singapore), don't stick the same person with always staying up late or getting up early. Rotate through time zones to keep things fair.
- Reorient how you organize your teams: We read horizontally so we tend to orient teams the same way. Instead, try organizing your teams vertically, from north to south. There might still be a lot of distance between team members, but the time zones will generally be closer together.
- Find the overlap: On most teams, you'll have one or two hours where working hours overlap—that's when you should meet. And getting everyone on camera for video calls helps build intimacy between coworkers regardless of proximity.
- Establish an agreed-upon time zone: You all might live across the globe, but the business has to be based somewhere. Avoid confusion and agree to always talk in one time zone.
- Record meetings: Given geographic limitations, not everyone will be able to make every meeting. Recording meetings captures the energy of the meeting and lets everyone feel included, whether they were there in real time or not. It also lets anyone review past discussions for greater clarity and any missed items.
- Double-check times: We all make mistakes, so use an online tool like one of these to get your time zones right: worldtimezone.com, worldtimebuddy.com, or timezoneconverter.com.
- Visualize time zones: Some of us need to see something for it to make sense. That's when an app like timezone.io comes in handy. On one screen, you can see where all of your teammates are in their time zone, anywhere in the world. And if you prefer graphs, check out everytimezone.com.

Just like with in-person or hybrid meetings, ask yourself if you really need to meet at all.

Collaborating in real time sometimes sounds better than it is, especially if someone has stayed up late or woken up early to attend.

Make sure the who, what, and why warrants everyone being there before people rearrange their schedules.

On our remote team, we often use apps like Loom to record video messages for each other. They let us easily share a video from our cameras and screens so we can explain new projects, SOPs (standard operating procedures), and other important information asynchronously—so regardless of what time someone's working, they get instant feedback and directions without needing to meet.

THE BOTTOM LINE

Meetings can be great or they can suck.

The best way to ensure they don't suck is to follow the recipe above and set your meetings up for epic success.

Don't start late, run late, or let the narcissistic drone down the hall hold everyone hostage—respect everyone's time and they will respect the meeting's structure in return.

Be communicative and transparent about why you are meeting, when, with whom, and what everyone needs to prepare before they get there.

Be equally clear about what you expect from people *after* the meeting—action items, deliverables and deadlines, and how and when they'll be accountable for their results.

Then have fun. Even introverts can enjoy a meeting when it has a purpose, is well run, and paced correctly.

CHAPTER RECAP

Most meetings are a waste of time—but they don't have to be.

The problem with most meetings is that they don't have a clear purpose, a concise agenda, or a simple process for capturing and following up on next steps.

You don't have to be a math whiz to figure out how much time is lost in just one needless hour-long meeting. Take the 60 minutes that you wasted and multiply it by the number of people in the room—suddenly that hour becomes 5 hours or even 10. And how many times does that happen each week?

While meetings have their place, there are many more efficient ways to update and collaborate with your team.

Messaging apps like Slack and project management apps like Asana can keep everyone on the same page—tracking progress, gathering opinions, assigning tasks, and distributing updates without pulling the whole company into the conference room or onto Zoom.

Apps like Loom let you record video messages for each other by capturing video from your camera and screen.

When meetings are the best way to get things done, here is the right way to hold them.

THE RECIPE FOR A PERFECT MEETING

- Only the people who need to be there, who have something to contribute, should be invited and attending. Don't pad the room with supporters, fans, or dead weight.
- Send the agenda 72 hours ahead, if you can. At a minimum, it must be in people's hands 24 hours before you meet.

Otherwise, people are spitballing during the meeting and you are not getting their best work.

- Attach any relevant resource materials to the agenda.
- 48 hours before the meeting takes place, conduct a roll call and make sure the right people have been invited. Use AI or other automation, email, or calls to confirm RSVPs and attendance.
- If a key person can't make it and they are critical to the meeting's success, reschedule to a time when everyone can be there. It is less expensive, time- and money-wise, to regroup than to plow ahead and then repeat the meeting when the pivotal person can rejoin.
- Every confirmed attendee should know the answers to these questions before they walk in the room:
  - Who's calling for the meeting?
  - Who's running the meeting?
  - Who else is attending?
  - How long is the meeting?
  - Where is the meeting being held?
  - Is it mandatory that I be there?
  - If my attendance is not mandatory, how will I add value by attending?
- Make sure the purpose of the meeting is spelled out in the invite, ideally in one sentence: Why are we meeting? What do we need to complete during the allotted time?
- Set time limits for every agenda item. This keeps the conversation laser-focused and reduces the impact of people repeating themselves or echoing a point already made.
- Clarify desired outcomes and assign roles in the agenda. Every meeting should have a timekeeper, an agenda keeper, a note taker, and a project manager to follow up on assigned tasks. These can be different people or the same person; what's important is that every role is assigned and everyone knows who's doing what and what they are accountable for.

- Start meetings on time and ensure everyone sticks to the time limits set for each topic on the agenda.
- If you're not done with a point when the time runs out, table that discussion until the next meeting.
- Appoint a meeting "project manager" to assign or record all action items, deliverables, and timelines, and get verbal confirmation before the meeting is over that everything is understood and agreed on. No one should leave the meeting unclear about next steps or who is responsible for them and by when.
- Never book back-to-back meetings. Always leave time before and after to shake off the last meeting and get ready for the next meeting. Brain science proves a small buffer between meetings reduces stress and improves focus. Eliminating back-to-back meetings also prevents anyone from running into your meeting late from a previous meeting.
- Within 24 hours after the meeting, send a concise, thorough recap to all attendees or publish the notes on a shared app, server, or drive. Send them also to anyone who wasn't there but who needs to be in the loop (stakeholders), or alert them on where to find the published notes.
- Debrief yourself after the meeting. Give yourself at least 15 minutes to schedule follow-up tasks in your calendar, update your to-do lists, read and revise any notes, and digest major takeaways and their implications.
- Engage any managers needed to ensure that all assigned tasks get done by their due dates.

Want to up your game a few notches and cover a ton of ground as quickly as possible? Here's a bonus item for you:

- Make attendees stand. This has a few benefits: It's harder for people to "multitask," and it ensures that no one gets so comfortable that they can't stay awake or on task.

Chapter 10
Social Media

"Social media is a double-edged sword. At its best,
offering unprecedented opportunities for marginalized
people to bring attention to their issues. At its worst,
allowing an unprecedented opportunity to be
outraged without reflection."
Roxane Gay

"Social media gives us this idea that we should all
have a posse of friends when in reality, if we have
one or two really good friends, we're lucky."
Brené Brown

Social media might feel like a convenient way to keep in touch, and it can be. But make no mistake—Big Tech has turned our basic desire for connection into a way to keep us engaged with *their platforms*, not other people, for longer and longer periods of time.

And while you scroll, they're scraping and mining every piece of data they can get their hands on to manipulate you in real time *and* strategically market to you in the future.

Between clickbait and meaningful connection, how much time are you spending on social media?

And are the connections there actively adding to the quality of your life, or are they just another waste of time?

If you're honest, you'll probably admit that social media is about 10 percent useful and 90 percent doomscrolling in pursuit of something engaging. Your mileage may vary, but it's no secret that the cons of social media can easily outweigh its positives.[51]

If you haven't yet watched *The Social Dilemma*, please do.[52] It pulls back the curtain on the evil geniuses who've engineered and perfected the art of putting our psyches into a vulnerable state with FOMO, and then flashing a supposed solution on the screen immediately afterward. Help is always just a click away!

By 2020, one study showed that the average adult spent three hours a day on social media.[53] The pandemic certainly didn't help that figure; TikTok exploded with 85 percent growth while our screens held us captive.[54]

Even one hour on social media per day—a lowball figure—wastes 365 hours a year, or the equivalent of nine working weeks.

And what do you get for that investment? Too often it's compromised mental health in the form of increased anxiety and depression.

One study found that engaging with Facebook led to a 7 percent increase in severe depression among college students. That's not a bad thing for Big Tech, because our happiness isn't their goal—holding our attention is.[55]

As the documentary *The Social Dilemma* also pointed out, our attention has become a hot commodity. Addiction is built right into the design.[56]

Which doesn't mean you can't or shouldn't use social media. But it *is* a time thief, and it can impact your mental health when not used carefully.

A FEW MORE PROBLEMS WITH SOCIAL MEDIA

Social media's sins are pretty widely understood, but it's still useful to list them:

- The time you spend on social media is time you aren't spending somewhere else. If all time is equal, what's the cost to you for every minute you spend there—especially if you're not using it for work?
- Because of how the algorithms work, you're often sent down rabbit holes or shown feeds that they want you to see—not the content you'd seek out from scratch. So the time is not only not optimized, it's often not even enjoyable.
- The content you're fed is specifically designed to foster FOMO. You'll never get your fill; there's always more content to serve you. And whatever gets a reaction from you—especially a negative reaction—means you'll see more of it. Just like sugar, alcohol, other drugs, and gambling, it's designed to keep you scrolling in search of the next jackpot. In fact, studies show that social media is like every addiction rolled into one highly toxic and accessible delivery system.[57] Well done, Silicon Valley!
- If you haven't yet turned off notifications, you can be interrupted constantly by updates and fresh content that is neither urgent nor important.
- It isn't just celebrities who look perfect in photos anymore; with countless filters and photo editing apps, now everyone can be skinny, tan, and glowing from the outside in. And even though you know it's a lie, it's still sometimes hard to see through the absurd representation that everyone's life is perfect except yours.
- It's nearly impossible to filter out the garbage from the content you're actually interested in. That's by design, too. So even when you jump onto social media with a specific

goal in mind, you're going to pay a price in the form of time lost as you claw your way out of the weeds.

- Without much regulation, bad actors regularly hijack these platforms and spread disinformation. We pay for this crap personally and as a society. Our social fabric is fraying every day from the cumulative effect of fake news and how that preys on the emotions of our gullible and less discerning friends, family, and colleagues. Not believing everything you read, see, or hear apparently doesn't apply to social media.

- I grew up when the only screen around was a TV, so I remember when real-world interactions were essentially the only interactions. We've got generations of digital natives now who can't distinguish between e-socializing and meeting IRL (in real life).

- Some of them are so screen-centric that they would do anything to avoid a phone call or a live interaction. And when they do meet in person, they often find it hard to put their devices down and make eye contact.

THE CONSEQUENCES

Many studies have been done on the consequences of social media, so here are just a few curated items:

- Overall use has a detrimental effect on mental health—lower self-esteem, reduced motivation, increased anxiety, and depression.
- You feel isolated and more lonely, not less.
- Your data is mined and sold to the highest bidder without your active consent.
- Based on your interests, you are fed certain ads and misinformation campaigns.
- You miss out on activities in real time when staring at a screen having FOMO about your friends' lives.

- You invest more time and energy in online relationships than real-life ones.
- You experience increased social awkwardness when you are actually around other people—feeling like every gesture and word is on display and being judged.
- You're constantly striving for an impossible ideal and the highly edited perfection you see in your feed, which isn't real.

In other words, spending time on social media is like binge-watching a show that makes you feel crappy about yourself.

Any benefits that come from social media are also available and generally more positive when they come via other forms of communication.[58] A quick phone call with a friend is a much more intimate and effective way to connect than liking their posts or making throwaway comments on Facebook.

HOW TO FIX IT

To neutralize social media's negative effects, you'll want to attack it on two fronts: technology and behavior/mindset.

TECHNOLOGY

- Turn off notifications and silence your devices. Without the constant dings and pings alerting you to new content, you'll be less likely to reach for your phone and get sucked into a social media wormhole. If you're worried you'll miss something important, pick one to two times each day to check your social media and follow up as needed.
- Unfollow anyone who doesn't add value to your life, or who you aren't actually interested in hearing from or about. Your feed can be a curated space that you control, as crazy as that sounds. If you don't like seeing posts from a certain person or business, unsubscribe, unfollow, or block them and move on.

- Use a "nanny" app that blocks social media access outside of preset windows of time. If you tend to be easily seduced by your TikTok feed or a particular Instagram influencer, these apps will keep you honest.
- If you're using social media for your business, be ethical in how you use it. There are plenty of ways to build and nurture an audience that doesn't exploit their vulnerabilities. It may take you longer than your competition to see results, but if you believe in people before profits, extend that position to include your social media practices, too.

BEHAVIOR/MINDSET

- Instant pudding isn't actually instant and it doesn't have to be, any more than your experience online has to be. Slow down and be deliberate about when, where, how, and why you do anything, particularly something as potentially addictive as social media.
- You actually don't have to be on social media. Many successful people aren't—and they would be if it made them happier or added something qualitative to their lives. Try a simple pro-and-con list and see how social media shows up in your life.
- If you decide to stay, establish rules for how and when you'll use it, and make sure those rules serve you and are not influenced by the platforms themselves. Remember they are designed to push your FOMO buttons relentlessly.
- Those rules, like your rules for email, should include specific check-ins at scheduled times of day. Break the habit of mindlessly scrolling whenever you have a few minutes to kill, because you don't have enough time to waste any of it.
- Decide what content and platforms you care about most, then be disciplined about checking those first. Set a timer for 15 minutes—and check off the important feeds and news before you start scrolling. When the timer goes off, stop and

assess whether to set it for another 15 minutes or if you've had enough for that session.

THE BOTTOM LINE

Social media, like any device that you use to interact with it, can be beneficial—if you are intentional about how you use it and realistic about what it is and how it functions.

If you view either as a toy or a game, you are sure to be met with an experience that confirms that and sucks you into using it more and more. Do not be naïve about how each have been deliberately engineered to exploit human psychology and biology.

Social media can connect us, but that is a red herring. It was designed to play off your vulnerabilities and exploit them for commercial gain. So any connection you feel is incidental to the larger, cumulative negative impact it has on your moods.

It was created to bait you with connection and then replace that with a deeper feeling of isolation to keep you on the platforms longer and longer.

If you're going to use social media, use it like you would any other controlled substance. Develop a set of rules around how and when you will get on and off it, and then stick to them.

You should also set expectations about your response time, especially if you use social media for your work.

Everyone is prey to internet trolls and other bad actors, but delays in either responding to or pulling down or hiding negative comments can have bigger consequences professionally than they would on a purely personal account.

CHAPTER RECAP

Big Tech has turned our basic desire for connection into a way to keep us engaged with *their* platforms—not other people—for longer and longer periods of time. While you scroll, they're scraping and mining every piece of data they can get their hands on to manipulate you in real time *and* strategically market to you in the future.

The average adult spends up to three hours a day on social media. Even one hour on social media per day—a lowball figure—wastes 365 hours a year, or the equivalent of nine working weeks.

And what do we get for our nine or more weeks of investment each year? Compromised mental health in the form of increased anxiety and depression.

HOW TO MAKE GOOD USE OF SOCIAL MEDIA

- Turn off notifications and silence your devices. If you're worried you'll miss something important, pick one or two times each day to check your social media and follow up as needed. Break the habit of mindlessly scrolling whenever you have a few minutes "to kill," because you don't have enough time to waste any of it.
- Unfollow anyone who doesn't add value to your life, or who you aren't actually interested in hearing from or about.
- Use a "nanny" app that blocks social media access outside of preset windows of time.
- If you're using social media for your business, be ethical in your use of it. There are plenty of ways to build and nurture an audience that doesn't exploit their vulnerabilities.
- You actually don't have to be on social media. Many successful people aren't! Try a simple pro-and-con list and see how or if social media adds value to your life.

- If you decide to stay on social media, establish rules for how and when you'll use it, and make sure those rules serve you.
- Decide what content and platforms you care about most, then be disciplined about checking those first. Set a timer for 15 minutes—and check off the important feeds and news before you start scrolling. When the timer goes off, stop and assess whether to set it for another 15 minutes or if you've had enough.

Chapter 11

Procrastination

"Procrastination is opportunity's assassin."
Victor Kiam

"It will never get easier. Start.
This moment is as good as it gets."
Sharon Pearson

Some people wear "procrastinator" like a dubious badge of honor—
"I am such a procrastinator," they say, as if they're both bragging and
complaining about it at the same time.

But, as with any self-deprecating remark, they're bragging and shaming
themselves at the same time.

I'm all for making light of something serious to blow up its intensity,
but saying things like this doesn't actually do that.

It just reinforces some of their 200 lies about their productivity and
their character and makes them feel like crap. Yuck.

So if you use that label, how does it serve you? Does it motivate you
to work harder? Or let you off the hook because, if you're such a
procrastinator, how could you possibly be expected to get anything
serious or important done?

Really, the way that we talk to ourselves sometimes is so screwed up.

And then we lump procrastination and laziness together like they're siblings or first cousins.

But let's be clear—procrastination is choosing to do one task over another as a way of delaying the inevitable. Laziness is choosing to do nothing.

Procrastination is almost always driven by avoidance.

You can dress it up and call it "self-care" by lingering longer on a task you're enjoying instead of pivoting to the thing you're supposed to do next . . . but avoidance is avoidance.

People have written about using procrastination to trick themselves into doing something they don't want to do by avoiding something they want to do even less.

But if you're looking to construct a simple life for yourself, those games seem like unnecessary busy-ness and mental gymnastics, right?

Do it or don't. Why burn through extra time and energy lying to yourself as well?

Procrastination is about delaying the inevitable—so what are you afraid of?

Maybe you're afraid of failing, of not knowing how to do something, of looking stupid, or of how long you think something will take to do.

Then you tell yourself one of your 200 lies—that you will definitely do this later, when you have more time.

I wish I had a dollar for every time a student in any of our coaching programs has said, "I can't believe I waited this long to do X, Y, or Z—I thought it was going take so long or be so hard. When I actually did it, it was so easy and took no time at all."

The trouble with procrastination is that it's a crappy long-term strategy. It doesn't get rid of things—it only slows them down.

Of course, you could be secretly hoping that the thing you're avoiding will eventually become obsolete. That sometimes happens—but most of the time, you're going to eventually have to do it.

HOW TO SPOT PROCRASTINATION

Learning to recognize procrastination is an important step toward defeating it, because sometimes a delay is just a delay.

You'll know you're procrastinating—as opposed to just taking awhile to get started—if you're doing one of two things: either avoiding something you don't want to do or indulging in something you are doing for too long.

AVOIDANCE
Willful avoidance looks like a looming deadline ahead and you deciding a bunch of other tasks are suddenly a lot more important. And those could be big or small: folding and putting the laundry away or finishing your taxes.

You tell yourself that you'll just get these things out of the way so you can really concentrate and then you'll dig into whatever you have to do to meet the deadline.

A telltale sign of subconscious avoidance is a biological need suddenly showing up. You're hungry or tired or really have to pee. You find it hard to concentrate on anything and tell yourself you'll just take a little nap and then, when you're fresh, you'll get right to it.

INDULGENCE

This is the one that masquerades as self-care and is driven by at least one of your 200 lies.

You just want to do the fun thing for five more minutes, because you never get to have fun anymore. Everything is work, work, work, and why shouldn't you take care of yourself and your own needs this one time?

The irony is that by indulging in this small pleasure you actually create more stress for yourself.

Your self-care is actually stolen time from the future that you're going to have to pay back with interest. You're not even free to enjoy what you're doing because you know something else is waiting for you.

HOW WE PROCRASTINATE

Deliberate self-sabotage doesn't sound good or feel good, so why do we do it?

Other than when our avoidance is so subliminal that we don't know we're doing it, most of the time we are well aware that something big is ahead. And while we should be attacking it, we've got a perfectly reasonable story for why we aren't, or aren't right now.

There are as many stories as there are people and tasks. At the same time, many of them look and sound quite familiar.

Here are a few of the best and most common excuses I've heard over the years. Do any of them sound familiar?

- "This feels too much like work."
- "They aren't paying me enough to work this hard."
- "If I wait long enough, it will just go away."
- "If I wait long enough, someone else will do it.
- "If I do this, something horrible will happen."
- "Why bother? No one ever gets what they want anyway."
- "I need to feel inspired to take on something like this."
- "I need more information before I take this on."
- "I would totally do this, but I don't know where to start."
- "I would totally do this, but I just don't see the value."
- "I would totally do this, but there isn't enough time."
- "I would totally do this, but I don't want to do it all alone."
- "I would totally do this, but I just can't afford to now."
- "I would totally do this, but only on my time and my terms."
- "There's too much riding on this. I can't take the pressure."
- "There's not enough time to get started."
- "There's not enough time to finish this."
- "You know me, I'm the worst procrastinator in the world."
- "It will take too long—I don't want to be doing this for years."
- "If I can't do it well, I don't want to do it at all."
- "If I start this, it's going to make things worse, not better."
- "As soon as I start this, so-and-so is going to get in my way. I don't want to start until they're out of the picture."
- "I'm tired. I'll get some rest and then I will totally start this."
- "I would rather die than do this if that's what so-and-so wants."
- "I'll do this tomorrow, I promise (or swear to God, or on my mother's grave, etc.)."
- "I'm just overwhelmed right now. Can't it wait?"
- "Do we really have to? I'd rather do something else right now."
- "I'm a free spirit. I don't believe in deadlines."
- "I totally forgot this was due . . . When is it due again?"
- "I work better under pressure anyway. I can always pull a rabbit out of my hat."

When you feel the urge to procrastinate, review this list and see if you've got a legitimate reason for putting something off or if you're just telling one of your 200 lies.

Chances are, if you can spot the story, you can poke a hole in it and get to work.

WHAT HAPPENS WHEN WE PROCRASTINATE

It may be obvious, but procrastination isn't only an inefficient coping mechanism. Sometimes the delays threaten our financial well-being, our physical or emotional health, our liberty, and sometimes even our lives.

To begin with, the thing that you want to spend the least amount of time with ends up being something you spend the most time with. Avoiding a task only saddles you with it until you eventually deal with it.

You're likely to miss opportunities if you've gained a reputation as someone who can't be trusted to complete projects on time.

You may miss out when something you're committed to drags on so long that you're unable to accept something new until the first task or project is finished.

You might suffer other damage to your reputation when word gets out. At best, people might label you a flake; and at worst, they might blackball you, preventing advancement at work or socially.

Whether or not other people talk about you, you may talk negatively to yourself about your procrastination, destroying your self-confidence and self-esteem.

Family members, friends, and partners may distance themselves from you as a result of your choices, leaving you isolated and alone.

Chronic procrastinators have been shown to have higher levels of stress than people who just suck it up and do things on time.[59]

That steady hum of low-level stress and anxiety playing in the background will make concentrating harder and remind you that you're avoiding something important.

Smaller tasks you're using to avoid doing something larger can take much longer. You might be worrying about what you have to do next or not be fully focused.

When you wait so long that you now have to scramble to meet a deadline, you create additional stress in a few ways—first from just trying to meet the deadline and then from trying to do your best in too little time.

The longer you wait to do something, the more complicated or expensive it may become.

The longer you wait to do something, the bigger or more important it might become in your imagination, even if it's not really that bad, or not bad at all.

Delaying tasks can impact stuff you enjoy doing—for example, having to leave later for a trip, return early, or reschedule it altogether.

You might also be doing the fun thing instead of the other thing, but you can't really relax and enjoy it because you know that as soon as you finish, you're going to have to do the thing you've been avoiding.

You might volunteer for other activities as a way of procrastinating and then start to resent what you're doing.

When we put things off that involve the law, finances, or the government, the consequences could be fines, loss of income, loss of reputation, loss of property, and even prison.

HOW TO FIX IT

The cure for procrastination is simple but not always easy. It just requires you to act.

Most people give procrastination more power and influence than it deserves. At some point, you probably just accepted that procrastination was inevitable or to be expected.

And while it doesn't often take a lot of planning to act, overcoming inertia requires a lot of energy all at once. Newton's First Law of Motion tells us that a body at rest tends to stay at rest until a significant force is applied.

Since this time thief is everywhere, the quickest way forward is to change your mindset first.

So if you've leaned on being a "chronic procrastinator" or applied any other labels to your habits in the past, you'll have to be willing to let them go or stay stuck where you are.

Procrastination is just a habit; it's not a part of your identity, like having brown eyes or being five feet nine.

You're also not special or extra broken or the "worst." You're just human.

Most, if not all, of us have done something similar at some point. Isolating yourself with any sort of label about your behavior will not serve you in changing that behavior.

Be honest: are you secretly trying to "win" being the worst at something because you're afraid your best isn't good enough . . . like Monica on *Friends* giving the best worst massages in the world?

Because procrastination is more like the time thief equivalent of Pennywise, the clown from Stephen King's *It*. As soon as you face your fears, it withers away. So here's how to banish it for good.

MINDSET CHANGES

Spend a few minutes reflecting on why you've been putting off a particular task. This exercise should not be used to procrastinate about doing something, so set a timer for no more than 10 minutes. That way you won't get lost down a rabbit hole.

There may be a pattern here and, if so, it can be useful to know that you often avoid similar kinds of tasks, like bookkeeping or cleaning up.

Then reconnect with why this task matters to you in the first place. If it's not important that you do it, just that it gets done, delegate it. If no one needs to do it, delete it.

Because there are only three ways to handle a task you're avoiding:

- Do it.
- Delegate it.
- Drop it.

That's it.

"Deferring it" is no longer an option. In fact, try this. Instead of saying "I am a procrastinator," replace that with this little mantra: "I don't defer, I deal."

Dealing with something doesn't mean you have to complete it immediately, of course. It just means you're no longer creating time clutter by kicking it down the road indefinitely.

So for every task that lands in your lap, you'll do one of three things—you'll decide when you're going to do it, you'll delegate it to someone else, or you'll drop it.

What you won't do is waste time playing with it, pushing it around, staring at it, and wishing it were gone.

It simply needs to be done by you, done by anyone, or not done at all.

I understand that it can be hard to "give up on your dreams" of learning French or how to knit, but if you haven't done either and you just keep moving them down your list, how badly do you actually want to do them?

If it matters to you, or you think it matters to you, take an action.

Sign up for an immersion class where you only speak French, or a knitting class, and see if you actually want to go further.

If nothing you can come up with to motivate yourself excites you, or they all feel like too much work, it's okay to let them go.

You're really only surrendering a story, since not learning French is no different than not going back to school to become a doctor. One may feel more fun, or closer and more achievable to you, but objectively they are equally remote.

When you keep these things around, they become another form of time clutter. They seem more important than they are because they've been around so long, but they don't really matter.

There is some sadness in accepting that you won't do something, in the way that there is always sadness when we accept a limitation or release something.

But the freedom you feel when you stop dragging crap around with you is so much sweeter and richer than any story you've been clinging to about being someone who will learn to speak French "someday."

Because even vague "someday" to-dos weigh you down and sap your energy.

BEHAVIORAL CHANGES
If you're not dropping it or delegating it, you're going to have to eat the frog.[60]

Mark Twain famously said, "Eat a live frog first thing in the morning and nothing worse will happen to you for the rest of the day." He also said, "And if it's your job to eat two frogs, it's best to eat the biggest one first."

And while you don't have to take this advice literally, it is the best weapon against procrastination.

So find the biggest task you've been procrastinating on—the worst thing in one of your time buckets—and make that your frog. It's usually not even that bad once you get started. It's just getting started that's the challenge.

If you do one a day, first thing in the morning, before life gets in the way, you'll eventually run out of frogs.

Set a timer for an hour, or two hours, or even three hours, and get it done before you do anything else.

And if it ends up only taking a few minutes, imagine how great you'll feel defeating the scariest monster before breakfast.

If you're avoiding a big project and aren't sure where to start, schedule some time to break it down into small, discrete steps. If you don't know how to break it into smaller steps, use the road map laid out for you in Chapter 7.

After you're up and dressed for the day, make it a habit to eat a frog before you even do your HVAs. Don't check your email, make a phone call, or sneak in a quick series of small tasks that "only take a minute." That's just more procrastination masquerading as productivity.

The cabinets have been waiting this long to be wiped down; they can wait another hour, right?

Likewise, now is not the time to prioritize self-care—other than eating the frog, which is really taking care of yourself.

A recent survey in the US shows that we're doing okay. On average, we actually only work 40-ish hours a week and get eight hours of sleep a night.[61]

So if you're thinking, "I'll just take a quick walk first—I need to get my steps in," that's one of your 200 lies. You can get your steps in when you finish eating the frog.

If you're thinking, "Eating the frog sounds too simple," you're almost right. It is simple. It's the thinking that complicates things.

When you build up procrastination into some towering mountain you have to climb, you're actually making it worse. But just like everything else, you climb that mountain one step at a time. And the first step is often the most difficult. Remember Mark LeBlanc and El Camino de Santiago.

Procrastination lives in your mind. At any moment, you can choose to do the thing. *You* are in charge, not this time thief.

When you understand that, procrastination will lose all of its power over you. For good.

THE BOTTOM LINE

Procrastination is built on fear—fear of how long something will take, what it will cost you, what you'll have to give up or have to deal with when you do the thing . . . story, story, story.

If anything, it's one of the least scary of the time thieves. It's mostly smoke and mirrors, so don't give it more power than it deserves.

And remember, winners do what they have to do—everyone else does what they want to do. So if you want to be a winner, whatever winning looks like for you, then you're going have to eat a few frogs.

Everyone can take one more step. For some things, it's the first step that matters.

Tap into the *why* for doing anything. It could need to be done for a good reason, but *you* don't have to do it. Great—delegate it.

And if you can't find the why, maybe it doesn't need to be done by anyone. Ever.

If you do have to do it, eat the frog. Now.

And remember Dr. Seuss's line: "Don't cry because it's over. Smile because it happened." That's a pretty perfect example of a glass-half-full mindset.

For more tips on eating the frog and kicking the shit out of procrastination, check out cbobbook.com/procrastination.

CHAPTER RECAP

Procrastination has a reputation for being the ultimate time thief.

Many of us wear procrastination as a badge of dishonor. "You know me, I'm *such* a horrible procrastinator!" We describe it as a personality trait rather than what it is: a less-than-useful habit.

Labels like that don't motivate us or serve us. They keep us stuck, losing hours to time thieves as though it were entirely out of our control.

To be clear, procrastination is simply choosing to do one task over another or choosing to do nothing as a way of delaying the inevitable. It is almost always driven by avoidance.

But when we avoid the things that we need or even want to do, we create a lot of needless complications and bring unnecessary pain into our lives.

One of the frustrating and sad ironies about procrastination is that the thing you want to spend the least time with often ends up being something you spend the most time with. And avoiding an inevitable task only saddles you with it until you eventually deal with it anyway.

Another consequence of procrastinating is missing out on opportunities or invitations if you've gained a reputation as someone who can't be trusted to complete tasks on time. You may also miss out when something drags on past its deadline and that prevents you from accepting a new project or assignment until the first task or project is completed.

If you've gained a reputation as someone who procrastinates, whether or not other people talk about you, you may talk negatively to yourself about your behavior, further eroding your self-confidence and self-esteem.

Whenever a delay requires you to scramble to meet a deadline, it creates additional stress. There is stress from trying to meet the approaching deadline and then more stress from trying to do your best in too little time.

The longer you wait to do something, the bigger, scarier, or more important it can become in your imagination, regardless of what's actually involved in starting or even finishing it.

The longer you wait to do something that you must do, the more complicated or expensive it may become in real life by the time you get around to doing it.

And when you put off things that involve the law, finances, or the government, the consequences could be fines, loss of income, loss of reputation, loss of property, and even prison.

Procrastination is almost always mental, meaning it lives inside your mind. If a physical limitation is not preventing you from doing something, you can find a way to address any emotional or psychological resistance you're experiencing.

Once you are clear that *you* are in charge, not this time thief, procrastination will lose all of its power over you. For good.

HOW TO STOP PROCRASTINATING

- The quickest way forward is to change your mindset. Procrastination is just a habit; it's not a permanent part of your identity.
- Spend a few minutes and reflect on why you've been putting off a particular task. There may be a pattern if you often avoid similar kinds of tasks, like bookkeeping, cleaning up, or correcting an employee.

- Reconnect with why a task matters to you in the first place. If it's not important that you do it, just that it gets done, delegate it. If no one needs to do it, delete it.
- There are only three ways to handle a task you're avoiding:
  - Do it.
  - Delegate it.
  - Delete it.
- For the tasks that you have to do, sometimes you can rely on Nike's "just do it" to get you into action. Other times, you're going to have to *eat the frog*. As Mark Twain famously said, eat a live frog first thing in the morning and nothing worse will happen to you for the rest of the day.
- To build some momentum, find a big task you've been avoiding—the worst thing in one of your time buckets—and make that your frog. It's usually not that bad once you get started; it's getting started that's the biggest challenge.
- Make it a habit to eat one frog a day, first thing in the morning, before you take on your HVAs or golf balls. Do this consistently, and you'll eventually run out of frogs.
- As with any other task, set a timer before you start eating your frog. That way, if you don't finish the frog, you won't feel stuck or like a failure. If the frog could not be completed in the allotted time, you'll have a better sense of how much more time you'll need to budget for that particular frog. And if it only takes a few minutes, imagine how great you'll feel defeating the scariest monster faster than you imagined.
- If you're avoiding a big project (or frog) because you aren't sure where to start, schedule some time to first break it down into small, discrete steps. If you need guidance on how to do this, use the road map laid out for you in Chapter 7.

Conclusion

By now, you've learned that time management is more a pervasive cultural myth than a tangible concept—like Santa Claus or the Tooth Fairy.

Time can't be managed; it moves forward without any help or hindrance from you. That knowledge should take some weight off your shoulders.

Time is also a great equalizer—everyone gets the same 168 hours every week. What you do with those hours is up to you.

And while you can't manage time, you *can* manage how you think about, feel about, and interact with time.

If that doesn't give you a sense of your own power to shape your destiny, nothing will.

Reading this book is a great place to start that journey.

In its pages, you've got all the concepts and tools you need to change your relationship with time for good.

And the biggest influence over becoming the most efficient, effective, productive, kick-ass version of yourself is your mindset.

Because the only difference between you and the world's most productive people are the decisions they make about their values and where they invest those 168 hours.

You didn't have to buy any fancy equipment, either. The three tools you need are right at your fingertips: a timer, a stopwatch, and your calendar.

You know now about the 8 Deadly Time Thieves, and you've got what you need to shut them down—a take-no-prisoners mindset and the willingness to eat the frog.

If you liked the book, I'm glad. Please tell everyone and leave me a positive review on Amazon and Goodreads.

Now you've got to take some action.

I've always loved this truism from British humorist Miles Kington: "Knowledge is knowing that a tomato is a fruit. Wisdom is not putting it in a fruit salad."[62]

So take your knowledge and turn it into wisdom by doing.

Ditch any lies, bullshit, and other baggage that holds you back while pretending to serve you.

Focus your time on your values and your wildly important goals—the things that make you *excited* to get out of bed in the morning.

I understand not being a morning person, even though I am one. But I don't understand not being excited to get out of bed and start the day, whenever that happens to be.

Clarity equals freedom. That's not super sexy or secret sauce-y, but it's true.

When you know what matters to you, what absolutely must get done, figure out how to get it done in whatever time you have, whether you have seven minutes a day like Sylvia Pettigrew or seven hours.

I put myself on the other side of the world to finish this book. I knew I needed to be far enough away from home that I could write all day and no one would be looking for me. I talked and texted with a few friends and family members, but I was parked in front of a computer, writing and revising.

The most important thing to me was getting this manuscript to the copyeditor by our deadline. Everything else could and did wait. And no one died.

So, whether you're all fired up and ready to put the actions in this book to work for you, or you're just starting to let yourself feel like *maybe* there's hope for you yet, I'm rooting for you.

I know you can do it because I can do it. And I am nothing special. Not in a falsely humble way—just in that I'm just another person. I'm not a person and a half. I don't have any superpowers.

I'm willing to do whatever it takes to get the things done that matter to me.

And I'm also honest with myself about accepting that some stuff won't get done.

I'm very careful about what that stuff is. I thoroughly consider what I'm not going to do as much as what I *am* going to do, so nothing rocks my world when it doesn't happen.

I love Joni Mitchell for so many reasons, and these words from the song "Both Sides Now" is one of them: "Something's lost, but something's gained in living every day."

Remember that those 200 lies—the ones floating around in the back of your head, telling you stories about how you aren't good enough, or how you can't because of your circumstances, or how this book was probably written for everyone except you—are all bullshit.

But if they can, those lies will find a way to creep back in.

And they're so devious because they know how to take a kernel of truth and twist it until it sounds plausible.

You may well have insane demands on your time. Some bosses and workplaces do suck. Some life circumstances are unfair and shitty.

Still, if you're going to get out of bed in the morning, and I sure hope you do, you're stuck with them until you change them.

Whatever your life looks like right now, it doesn't have to stay that way.

In 1989, I stopped drinking and self-medicating. That had been my way of dealing with what I thought was the shitty hand of cards I had been dealt.

I made a commitment to pay attention and take responsibility for everything in my life from that day forward.

And that one promise has changed literally everything else about my life to this day.

Shit will happen . . . it does happen.

The solution is paying attention and meeting whatever arises as it arises.

If it doesn't kill you, you have an opportunity to try again.

I hope that I always choose any discomfort that comes with living in reality over the pain those 200 lies are cooking up for me. Smells delicious, tastes like shit.

Be grateful for whatever is currently present in your life, because you chose it. Possibly while sleepwalking, but it's still yours. If you don't want it, pack it up and drop it off at the nearest thrift store so someone else can use it.

And if it's just trash, get rid of it so no one else ends up with it.

What do you want right now? What does a life free of stress, anxiety, rushing around like a crazy person, and second-guessing every decision look like for *you*?

Because everything you need to get there, from fundamental concepts to practical tools, is both in your hands, and more importantly, in your head and heart at this very moment.

You've got those ruby slippers on your feet, too—don't waste them.

It's been a while since I've done drag, but for you, if it's helpful to imagine me as Glinda the Good Witch, I'll do it.

If and when you do find yourself sliding back into time chaos—and there's no shame in that, we all do it—it's okay.

Just get back on your feet and take one more step.

And if you are a type A person, please don't try to implement every strategy in this book instantly. You'll make yourself and everyone around you nuts.

Tackle one time thief at a time. Use one, two, or three of the strategies that seem easiest and make the most sense to you. If you are diligent and deliberate and consistent, you *will* see measurable and significant results fast.

You don't need to go from one to 100 in a single leap. Just getting from one to 10 is a 10-fold improvement.

If you're feeling overwhelmed or lost and need to find true north, go back to your values. What matters most to you? How close to or far from alignment with them are you right now?

Most people bail on themselves because they'd rather be comfortable than really, truly happy. Or miserable and content knowing that at least they tried and that their misery is a result of their own choices.

Like in the fable of the fox and the grapes, they tell themselves that either what they have is good enough or they didn't really want it anyway.

But you and I both know that simmering under that line of bullshit is a deeper truth: they either don't know what's important to them or have just given up believing that they can be happy, too.

Remember this—if your choices have the power to make you miserable today, they also have the power to make you insanely happy tomorrow.

So what's it going to be: short-term "comfort" or a life beyond your wildest dreams?

No bullshit—the choice is completely up to you.

Acknowledgments

It's been more than a decade since my first book, *Unstuff Your Life!*, came out. For everyone who helped launch it, my gratitude still stands. Many of the same people have continued to support me in bringing this latest book and my work in general further into the world. I'm sure I seldom express my appreciation adequately for their ongoing kindness. Many more people have encouraged me since *Unstuff Your Life!* was published, and I hope to remain worthy of their generosity.

This book would not exist without the talent and tenacity of Sarah Kuiken, Carra Simpson, Erin Parker, Kristy Twellmann Hill, Jazmin Welch, and Merrie-Ellen Wilcox. I met Carra Simpson through the fantastic Susan Piver—friend, colleague, author, and luminous soul. Thanks, Seth Godin, for the intro.

The current team at AMI (Andrew Mellen, Inc.)—including my friend and colleague Kevin Smith, my extraordinary assistant Kristin Hart, Facebook ads wizard Luke Nevill, and virtual assistant Ven Juliene Corpuz—makes everything possible. Shout-outs to past members Awilda Acosta, Kelly Case, Alice Chin, Michelle Dellavalle, John Gugliada, Maya D. Haynes, Drew Jacobsen, and Paula Thrall—each played a meaningful role in getting us here today.

Literary and real-life friend Tyson Cornell has been a wealth of knowledge and heart, and you're reading this partly because he helped get this book seen and into your hands.

As always, continued respect and appreciation for literary agent James Levine and the excellent team at LGR Literary Agency.

I've repeatedly tapped into the wisdom of Jenifer Madson, Sheri Rosenthal, Gaylord Neely, James P. Friel, and Yara Golden—thanks for always answering the call.

Visionary entrepreneurs Brad Stevens and Bubba Levy have been instrumental in our working with several YPO (Young Presidents' Organization) and EO (Entrepreneurs' Organization) chapters so far—thanks for seeing value in the work and helping expand its reach and impact.

A big shout out to all current and past members of our coaching programs: the Unstuff Your Life System, Your Next BIG Thing and De-Stress Your Mess Challenge. You all have taught me as much as I've taught you and I'm deeply grateful for your commitment, enthusiasm, and trust.

Props to Fabienne Fredrickson, her husband Derek Fredrickson, and the entire BoldHeart community. I met my dear friend and accountability buddy Victoria Whitfield there, along with many other talented and big-hearted business leaders—notably Denise Allen, Lorry Leigh Belhumeur, Rebekah Marler, Rucsandra Mitrea, Lisa Poulson, Niki Rubinger, and Charisse Sissou. Thanks for the camaraderie and shared vision of excellence.

Ditto members of the Experts Collective: Mario Armstrong, Wendy Diamond, Thomas Farley, Pauline Frommer, Michael Green, Alastair Greer, Roshini Rajapaksa, Amy Salinger, and Andrea Syrtash.

I am lucky I get to speak all over the world. Kathy Harris and the SHRM Speakers Bureau have been great champions. Fellow travelers on the road who make it better include Warren Knight, Scott Friedman, Jana Stanfield, and the evolving community of Together We Can Change the World.

Likewise, I get to teach each year at Rancho La Puerta, and for that, deep appreciation to George Fahouris, Barry Shingle, Victoria Larrea, Deborah Szekely, Sarah Livia Brightwood, and the entire staff and extended RLP family.

Speaking of family, a few relatives need acknowledgment: my mom, Frances Mellen; "aunt" Sandy Efros; and cousins Elyse Kaps, Irene Krinsky, Susan Turetsky, Marc Rosenblatt, Lauren Turetsky, Shea Cohen, Andrea Wilber Marcus, David Kosins, and Stuart Wilber and his partner, John Breitweiser.

In alphabetical order, these friends and colleagues deserve so much more than their names listed here, but this will have to do for now: Chef AJ, Don Alden, Debra Amerson and Barbara Hoefle, Ed Bacon, Michelle Battista, Darrin Bodner, Laurie Brown, Sarah Byam, Johnny Caruso, Robert Charron, Walker Clark, Tamsen Fadal, Sallie Fraenkel, Jill Finsen, Susan Finsen, Beth Garr, Phil Gerbyshak, Mitch Goldstone, Michael Gonzalez-Wallace, Jaime Grant, Marcia Griffin, Amy Gross, Judith Helfand, Stewart Hopkins and Nancy Werner, Gabrielle and Rey Horowitz-Prisco, Peter Hurley, Micki Hurwitz, Randy Kaufman, Stephanie Kelly, George Kimmerling & Larry Kressley, Carolyne Landon, Richard Lang and Judith Selby Lang, Mark LeBlanc, Richard Linebaugh, Linda Lippner, Chuck London, Jennifer Louden, Michael MacLennan, Patricia Mills, Quinn Morgan, Casey Nelson, Ellen Yogacharya O'Brian, Roberta Rockwell, Phil Rossiello, Tina Sabuco and Shellye Arnold, Sharon Salzberg, Skip Scheetz, Nancy Stern, Wendy Stevens, David Stewart, Dr. Sé Sullivan, Mia Tagano and John Malloy, Nicole "Jade" Ullmann, Peter Walsh, Joyce Ellen Weinstein, Jennifer White, Rosalind Wiseman, and Michael Woody.

A few people kept me afloat years ago in Seattle. Although they are gone, their support at a low point in my life remains. RIP Cheryl Cebula, John Mifsud, and Lynne McGinty.

My many clients continue to shape and inform this work and the information in this book. To avoid false modesty, excessive name-dropping, and violating their privacy, I'll simply acknowledge them all here without naming names, with one exception—the IIABA. A big shout out to a few members of its leadership team: Jennifer Becker, Susie Bonner, and Leslie Mularski, and the many CEOs and education directors who have invited me to their chapters. Thank you all for your curiosity and willingness to implement change even when story, reticence, and resistance also crop up—way to walk the walk.

No doubt I have forgotten many other people who inspire me to get up and dig in for one more day. For that, please forgive my poor memory. Any omissions reflect solely on me and not on your influence or significance. Either way, let's continue walking together, one moment at a time, with as much grace as we can muster, along with a bit less frenzy. After all, busy is just bullshit, right?!

Endnotes

1   Andrew Mellen, "200 Lies a Day and Counting!," August 9, 2017, https://www.andrewmellen.com/post/7-200-lies-a-day-and-counting.

2   "Eric Brenn 'Plate Spinning' on The Ed Sullivan Show," filmed June 15, 1958, video, 1:29, https://www.youtube.com/watch?v=Cb6NS_F5xTE.

3   "Average Person Lies 200 Times per Day," myGC, September 26, 2019, https://www.mygc.com.au/average-person-lies-200-times-per-day.

4   Ellen Barry, "Can This Man Stop Lying?" *New York Times,* November 29, 2022, https://www.nytimes.com/2022/11/29/health/lying-mental-illness.html.

5   Madhuleena Roy Chowdhury, "The Neuroscience of Gratitude and Effects on the Brain," Positive Psychology, April 9, 2019, https://positivepsychology.com/neuroscience-of-gratitude/.

6   "The Science of Mindfulness," Mindful, August 31, 2022, https://www.mindful.org/the-science-of-mindfulness/.

7   Discipline Equals Freedom, "If You Go to the Gym and Don't See Results," February 7, 2022, video, 0:45, https://youtube.com/shorts/0QIF0iQwHS8.

8   Meir Kay, "A Valuable Lesson for a Happier Life," May 4, 2016, video, 3:05, https://www.youtube.com/watch?v=SqGRnlXplx0.

9   McKenna Princing, "This Is Why Deep Breathing Makes You Feel So Chill," Right as Rain, September 1, 2021, https://rightasrain.uwmedicine.org/mind/stress/why-deep-breathing-makes-you-feel-so-chill.

10   Leigh Beeson, "Some Types of Stress Could Be Good for Brain Func-
      tioning," UGA Today, July 28, 2022, https://news.uga.edu/some-stress
      -is-good-for-brain-function/.

11   Christophe André, "Proper Breathing Brings Better Health," *Scientific
      American,* January 15, 2019, https://www.scientificamerican.com/
      article/proper-breathing-brings-better-health/.

12   Mike Robbins, "Is Your Attention on Your Intention? How to Create
      the Life You Really Want", Oprah.com, accessed December 23, 2022,
      https://www.oprah.com/spirit/setting-and-achieving-goals-with-
      intention/all.

13   Cal Newport, "The 3-Hour Fields Medal: A Slow Productivity Case
      Study," July 5, 2022, https://www.calnewport.com/blog/2022/07/05/
      the-3-hour-fields-medal-a-slow-productivity-case-study/.

14   Keri Wiginton, "Your Ability to Focus May Be Limited to 4 or 5 Hours
      per Day. Here's How to Make the Most of Them," *The Washington Post,*
      June 1, 2021, https://www.washingtonpost.com/lifestyle/wellness/
      productivity-focus-work-tips/2021/05/31/07453934-bfd0-11eb-b26e
      -53663e6be6ff_story.html.

15   Anna Powers, "Failing Your Way to Success: Why Failure is a Crucial
      Ingredient for Success," *Forbes,* April 30, 2018, https://www.forbes.
      com/sites/annapowers/2018/04/30/failing-your-way-to-success-why
      -failure-is-a-crucial-ingredient-for-success/?sh=661fecbb6170.

16   "Planning fallacy," Wikipedia, accessed December 23, 2022, https://
      en.wikipedia.org/wiki/Planning_fallacy.

17   Brené Brown, "Shame vs. Guilt," January 15, 2013, https://brene-
      brown.com/articles/2013/01/15/shame-v-guilt/.

18   Peter Economy, "A New Study of 19 Million Meetings Reveals that
      Meetings Waste More Time Than Ever (but There IS a Solution)," Inc.,
      January 11, 2019, https://www.inc.com/peter-economy/a-new-study
      -of-19000000-meetings-reveals-that-meetings-waste-more-time-than
      -ever-but-there-is-a-solution.html.

19   James Clear, *Atomic Habits: An Easy and Proven Way to Build Good
      Habits and Break Bad Ones* (New York: Avery, 2018).

20   Jonathan B. Spira and Joshua B. Feintuch, "The Cost of Not Paying
      Attention: How Interruptions Impact Knowledge Worker Produc-

tivity" (Basex, September 2005), https://iorgforum.org/wp-content/uploads/2011/06/CostOfNotPayingAttention.BasexReport1.pdf.

21   Christine Carter, "Please Stop Interrupting Me!," *Greater Good Magazine*, June 24, 2015, https://greatergood.berkeley.edu/article/item/please_stop_interrupting_me.

22   Sara Novak, "Investigating Screen Time's Impact on the Attention Span," *Discover*, December 9, 2021, https://www.discovermagazine.com/mind/investigating-screen-times-impact-on-the-attention-span.

23   Jia Wertz, "Open-Plan Work Spaces Lower Productivity and Employee Morale," *Forbes*, June 30, 2019, https://www.forbes.com/sites/jiawertz/2019/06/30/open-plan-work-spaces-lower-productivity-employee-morale/?sh=435fd5b861cd.

24   Jiaa Haomiao and Erica I. Lubetkin, "Life expectancy and active life expectancy by marital status among older US adults: Results from the U.S. Medicare Health Outcome Survey (HOS)," *SSM - Population Health* 12 (December 2020), https://doi.org/10.1016/j.ssmph.2020.100642.

25   "Multitasking: Switching Costs," American Psychological Association, accessed December 23, 2022, https://www.apa.org/topics/research/multitasking.

26   Kevin P. Madore and Anthony D. Wagner, "Multicosts of Multitasking," *Cerebrum* 2019 (Mar–Apr 2019), https://www.ncbi.nlm.nih.gov/pmc/articles/PMC7075496/.

27   Karen Pace, "The Myth of Multitasking: Research Says It Makes Us Less Productive and Increases Mistakes," Michigan State University, March 31, 2017, https://www.canr.msu.edu/news/the_myth_of_multitasking_research_says_it_makes_us_less_productive_and_incr.

28   "Distracted Driving," NHTSA, accessed December 24, 2022, https://www.nhtsa.gov/risky-driving/distracted-driving

29   Edgar Snyder, "Texting and Driving Accident Statistics," Edgar Snyder & Associates, accessed December 24, 2022, https://www.edgarsnyder.com/car-accident/cause-of-accident/cell-phone/cell-phone-statistics.html.

30   Christopher Chabris and Daniel Simons, "Selective Attention Test," filmed 1999, video, 1:22, http://www.theinvisiblegorilla.com/gorilla _experiment.html.

31   Vanessa Loder, "Why Multi-Tasking Is Worse Than Marijuana for Your IQ," *Forbes*, January 11, 2014, https://www.forbes.com/sites/ vanessaloder/2014/06/11/why-multi-tasking-is-worse-than-marijuana -for-your-iq.

32   Curt Steinhorst, "How Multitasking Erodes Productivity and Dings Your IQ," *Forbes*, February 20, 2020, https://www.forbes.com/sites/ curtsteinhorst/2020/02/20/how-multitasking-erodes-productivity -and-dings-your-iq/?sh=60e4fa423b7e.

33   "Dopamine and serotonin: Brain chemicals explained," Medical News Today, accessed December 24, 2022, https://www.medicalnews today.com/articles/326090.

34   Judson Brewer, *Unwinding Anxiety: New Science Shows How to Break the Cycles of Worry and Fear to Heal Your Mind* (New York: Penguin Random House, 2021), page 28.

35   "Over-Commitment Epidemic: 3 out of 5 People Say They Can't Possibly Get Everything Done on Their To-Do List," PR Newswire, January 23, 2019, https://www.prnewswire.com/news-releases/over -commitment-epidemic-3-out-of-5-people-say-they-cant-possibly-get -everything-done-on-their-to-do-list-300782549.html.

36   Henri-Frédéric Amiel, *The Journal of Henri-Frédéric Amiel*, (Lausanne, Suisse: Éditions l'Âge d'Homme, 1994), page 325.

37   Mary Oliver, *New and Selected Poems, Volume One* (Boston: Beacon Press, 1992), 94.

38   Andrew Mellen, "Unstuff Your Life System," accessed December 24, 2022, https://www.andrewmellen.com/uyls.

39   Francisco Sáez, "The Science Behind GTD," FacileThings, accessed December 26, 2022, https://facilethings.com/blog/en/science.

40   Dale Carnegie, *How to Stop Worrying and Start Living* (New York: Simon & Schuster, 1984), page 37

41   Matt Plummer, "How to Spend Way Less Time on Email Every Day," *Harvard Business Review*, January 22, 2019, https://hbr.org/2019/01/ how-to-spend-way-less-time-on-email-every-day. Note: Assuming

the math in the article is based on a standard workday rather than a whole day, 8 hours x 60 minutes/hour = 480 minutes. Divide that by 15 email checks, and you get an email check every 32 minutes, rather than every 37, as stated in the article. While Mr. Plummer's math is off, the research referenced in the article is accurate.

42   Kostadin Kushleve and Elizabeth W. Dunn, "Checking Email Less Frequently Reduces Stress," *Computers in Human Behavior* 43 (February 2015): 220–28, https://doi.org/10.1016/j.chb.2014.11.005.

43   Plummer, "Less Time on Email."

44   Susan Greenfield, "You've Got Mail," *Psychology Today*, January 26, 2015, https://www.psychologytoday.com/us/blog/mind-change/201501/youve-got-mail.

45   Kabir Sehgal, "How to Write Email with Military Precision," *Harvard Business Review*, November 22, 2016, https://hbr.org/2016/11/how-to-write-email-with-military-precision.

46   James Spillane, "Work Meetings Are Destroying Business (and How to Destroy Them Back)," Business2Community, March 2, 2016, https://www.business2community.com/human-resources/work-meetings-destroying-business-destroy-back-01471046.

47   Nina Paczka, "Meeting in the Workplace | 2022 Statistics," LiveCareer, July 25, 2022, https://www.livecareer.com/resources/careers/planning/workplace-meetings-2022-statistics.

48   "Research Proves Your Brain Needs Breaks," Microsoft, April 20, 2021, https://www.microsoft.com/en-us/worklab/work-trend-index/brain-research.

49   Jeff Haden, "New Research: Fewer Meetings Boosts Employee Productivity, Communication, and Job Satisfaction," Inc., accessed December 26, 2022, https://www.inc.com/jeff-haden/new-research-shows-holding-fewer-meetings-boosts-employee-productivity-communication-job-satisfaction.html.

50   Economy, "A New Study of 19 Million Meetings."

51   Frances Dalomba, "Pros and Cons of Social Media," Lifespan, March 1, 2022, https://www.lifespan.org/lifespan-living/social-media-good-bad-and-ugly.

52   *The Social Dilemma*, directed by Jeff Orlowski-Yang (Los Angeles, California: Netflix, 2020), https://www.thesocialdilemma.com/.

53   Catherine Hiley, "Screen time report 2022," Uswitch, September 13, 2022, https://www.uswitch.com/mobiles/screentime-report/.

54   S. Dixon, "Social Media Use during COVID-19 Worldwide: Statistics and Facts," Statista, October 18, 2022, https://www.statista.com/ topics/7863/social-media-use-during-coronavirus-covid-19-worldwide/ #dossierKeyfigures.

55   Dylan Walsh, "Study: Social Media Use Linked to Decline in Mental Health," MIT Sloan School of Management, September 14, 2022, https://mitsloan.mit.edu/ideas-made-to-matter/study-social-media -use-linked-to-decline-mental-health.

56   Mike Brooks, "The 'Vegas Effect' of Our Screens," *Psychology Today*, January 4, 2019. https://www.psychologytoday.com/us/blog/tech -happy-life/201901/the-vegas-effect-our-screens.

57   "The Social Dilemma: Social Media and Your Mental Health," McLean Hospital, December 2, 2022, https://www.mcleanhospital.org/ essential/it-or-not-social-medias-affecting-your-mental-health.

58   Brittany Edelmann, "Social Media May Be Changing the Way You Communicate," *Discover*, October 27, 2022, https://www.discover magazine.com/technology/social-media-may-be-changing-the-way -you-communicate.

59   Julie Marks, "Effects of Procrastination: The Good and the Bad," PsychCentral, updated July 24, 2022, https://psychcentral.com/ health/good-and-bad-things-about-procrastination.

60   Brian Tracy, "Eat That Frog: Brian Tracy Explains the Truth About Frogs," accessed December 30, 2022, https://www.briantracy.com/ blog/time-management/the-truth-about-frogs/.

61   Susan Cullen, "Startling Statistics About How We Spend Our Time," Nexa Learning, January 17, 2022, https://www.nexalearning.com/ blog/bid/50652/startling-statistics-about-how-we-spend-our-time.

62   Miles Kington, https://www.goodreads.com/quotes/184158-know ledge-is-knowing-that-a-tomato-is-a-fruit-wisdom.

About the Author

Photo by: Peter Hurley

ANDREW MELLEN is a speaker and coach, and the author of the *Wall Street Journal* bestseller *Unstuff Your Life!* and *The Most Organized Man in America's Guide to Moving*. He is the creator of the De-Stress Your Mess Challenge, the Unstuff Your Life System, and the Calling Bullsh*t on Busy Mastermind—virtual programs that have helped over 500,000 people and businesses around the world change their relationships with stuff, time, and clutter for good.

Mellen has been a student of mindfulness and meditation since 1989. In a previous career, he was an award-winning actor, director, and arts administrator who toured the United States performing improvisational theater in prisons and penitentiaries. He currently splits his time between New York, Lisbon, Southeast Asia, and Treasure Island, Florida.

Keep in Touch

Did you benefit from *Calling Bullsh*t on Busy*?

SHARE YOUR PRAISE

Did this book help you get more time in your day? Did it offer new insights into time management that are benefiting your daily life and relationships?

If so, a review, shared through your favorite online retailer, would be greatly appreciated! A few minutes of your time could help others find this book and enjoy some of the benefits you've already received.

PLACE A BULK ORDER

Would you like to share this book with your company, team, group, or class? We offer bulk discounts for orders of 10 or more copies in most locations. Write to hello@andrewmellen.com.

WORK WITH ANDREW

Even better, would you like Andrew to speak or train at your organization, conference, book club, or event? Write to speak@andrewmellen.com.

KEEP IN TOUCH

For more about Andrew's books, programs, and workshops, please visit andrewmellen.com.

Once you're there, be sure to register for upcoming De-Stress Your Mess Challenges, the Calling Bullsh*t on Busy Mastermind, as well as other events and opportunities to simplify your life and maximize your time.

Also by Andrew Mellen

Unstuff Your Life! Kick the Clutter Habit and Completely Organize Your Life for Good

Available in paperback, ebook, and audio
New edition coming Fall 2023

"The Most Organized Man in America" shows readers how to kick the clutter habit, step by step, in his complete guide to getting and staying organized . . . for good!

The Most Organized Man in America's Guide to Moving

Available in paperback and ebook
October 2019

Moving house doesn't have to stress you out or overwhelm you ever again! Get step-by-step instructions, including a master checklist, from America's favorite organizer in this compact, foolproof guide.

Printed in Great Britain
by Amazon

32356607R00178